Christmas Letters

by Mark Mendizza

Larissa Press
Laguna Niguel, California

ISBN 978-1-7375107-0-3 (paperback)

First Edition

The Library of Congress Cataloging-in-Publication Data is available upon request.

Book design & graphics: Brian Ziegler

Published in the United States of America

To Sue and Lara

Where the magic begins

A family without a funny Christmas letter is like a bird without a song.

— Mark Mendizza

Contents

Preface

The Christmas Letter
Respected – Neglected – Resurrected

For 25,000 years the Christmas letter has been a respected epistolary art. The ancient cave paintings at Lascaux are considered by some experts to be the result of a few prehistoric parents bragging about their kids and boasting about how many bison they were able to kill with a stick—in short, a Christmas letter. Examined closely, it is also clear that the Egyptian hieroglyphics on the walls of the Great Pyramids are actually Christmas letters, a "whassup in the empire" for Pharaoh's friends, family, and the gods. And although everyone knows that the Bible was the first imprint on Gutenberg's new press, only a few know that the second project was a Christmas letter, a beautiful work dedicated to his daughter's first dance recital.

In our time, however (since TV and two-working-parent households), the high art of the Christmas letter has been neglected, drifting from its august origins into short, cursory accounts of kids hitting home runs in Little League, pet stories, and anecdotes about camping trips. *People!* Our lives are deeper, richer and worthy of more than a few cursory remarks about grade level and lies about how well your job is going. Which is precisely why we have published *The Christmas Letters*. By including more poignant and funny details than anyone but grandparents and a few federal agents would ever want to know about our family, we hope to resurrect the lapsed status of the Yuletide epistolary tradition, to link our humble history with yours, and finally to maybe get a humiliating spot on *YouTube.*

Hundreds of people have already found the *Letters* to be funny, touching, and, like our family itself, downright daffy. At first, our friends were as shocked as you will be by the audacity, hilarity and length of *The Christmas Letters,* but gradually the charm and enchantment began to grow on them. And now they want

Easter Letters, Labor Day Letters, and *Letters* for each solstice.

Together, the eleven letters represent a humorous effort to recall for ourselves, friends, relatives and of course you (plus some famous people we're stalking), the spirit of our lives and times, year by year, one humbling incident after another over the last decade. As we bid adieu to the 90's AND the Millennium, we hope you will think of this little history as our way of reaching out to yours; as a celebration of the forgiving spirit of Christmas and of our rich, common heritage: the universal heritage of human beings getting through the day together. Read the letters together with your own family and you will grow closer. Give them to friends, and they will loan you money. Let them inspire your own appreciation for the precious moments that too often slip unnoticed, and at the same time pay for our cosmetic surgery. It is time to return the Christmas Letter to its rightful place in the literary pantheon, which, if you feel anything like we do, should be somewhere within reach of the commode. Honor the little things in your lives, especially the kids.

And may Christmas be with you forever.

Mark & Sue

The Year of the Dog

Mark, Sue and Fergie
Long Beach, California

December 1988

Dear Friends and Family,

OK, guess what we DID this year! No. No lifts. No liposculpting. Not yet. We didn't get personal trainers, either, thus avoiding anything like results. We did find a new colon cleanser, but that's not it. And we didn't have affairs. I mean we just got married, for crying out loud. Why would you think like that? No. We didn't do anything tawdry and you should be ashamed of yourself for even thinking such a thing about Sue and me. I mean this is a Christmas letter, for Christ's sake, and Sue and I are still totally in love.

As you know, we were married in 1987. We spent most of 1988 figuring out whose furniture to keep, and establishing boundaries for our "personal space." Let's see, do we keep the cinderblock bookshelf and apple crates from my stuff, or use Sue's hardwood armoires from the Italian Renaissance. Hmmm? To help you visualize our personal space allotment, think of our bathroom as the European continent. Now, think of the state of Liechtenstein. Got it? I get Liechtenstein, and Sue gets the rest of Europe, plus the People's Republic of China.

Which brings us to Christmas 1988. Have you guessed what we did yet? Give up? OK: this year we went a little crazy, way outside the envelope, as they say. Yes, we bought a dog. A little brown barking dog. It was a big move for Sue and me, and it's been somewhat transformative. To us, the dog has been like a beta version of a kid, a child, if you know what we mean. What we really did this year was take the very first step, at least in our own minds, toward becoming parents. Not really, of course, but sort of.

Right now, we're way too busy, tentative, and scared to have a baby. First of all, because we're not really young people any more, like so many parents we see around our neighborhood. In the morning we hear them going to work. All the garage doors on the street creak open at exactly the same time. We peek out our window and see the young men walk out their front doors in their spiffy Suits-R-Us suits, briefcases in hand. They kneel down and hug the kids, then they kiss their wives. Then they all get on their skateboards and push off to work. "They seem so young," I whisper to Sue. "Not really," she says. "People are just maturing later than they used to." "If we have a baby now," I say, "when it turns eighteen, I will be a hundred and seven." "We'll stay young," she consoles. "We'll get trainers."

The dog idea came out of nowhere. After having been married for about three minutes, I remember we started saying things like this: "Do you want a child?" "I don't know, do you?" "Yes, well it's sort of an important part of life, isn't it?" "Well, yes. I think it is, but there are other things in life that are important, too." "Sure there are." "Like the beach and stuff." "Yeah." "Do you think we are ready to take care of a child?" "I don't know. What do you have to do?" "Feed it, first of all, I guess." "Can we feed a baby?" "Maybe we should get a dog first; see if we can keep a dog alive." "Yeah. Let's do that." "Yeah. What kind of dog do you think?" We figured that if we could feed a dog once or twice a day for a whole year that would mean we had what it takes to raise a child. It was a test. Sue saw an ad in the paper for a dachshund, if you can believe that: a miniature dachshund, no less. She called the number and drove right over on a Monday morning I think it was.

I stayed home. I was supposed to be working. As you know, I call myself a writer-producer. It has a nice ring to it, but it's a stretch, slightly hyperbolic, but aren't we all? Full of stretch and hyperbole. My Uncle Bob would say we're full of something else. I was supposed to be writing an article about titanium bolts that were dramatically decreasing weight ratios for a new bicycle drive train, enabling cyclists in the Tour de France to make a proportional reduction in their use of illegal steroids. That's what I do. I help big companies discover and tell their stories, so people will buy their products.

But instead of writing about the new crank bolts, I was reading about dark matter. It's something that has concerned me ever since I found out about it, maybe ten years ago. Until we find out the truth about dark matter, we won't know whether the ultimate destiny of the universe will be to continue to expand infinitely outward and eventually become so big and cold that only lawyers could live in it; or, if there's enough dark matter, to collapse back—from the collective force of gravity—into the dense little ball, like the size of a pea or something, from which it supposedly banged. (See: Big Bang). Can you imagine all the matter in the universe condensing down to the size of a bee-bee, which is how big it was just before the big bang broadcast everything out to the ends of the—well, you can't say that; you can't say broadcast everything out to the ends of the universe because there wasn't really a universe there yet. Instead of working, I'm pondering this dilemma. I'm thinking about what it would be like living in a space that small, not only with all the matter in the universe crowding in upon your own "personal" space, but relatives and all kinds of ethnic groups as well. The phone rings and a jolt, like the one I get from mail that has Internal Revenue anywhere on the envelope, runs through my body. I get a minor whiplash, which is typical of my spastic reaction to reality. Whenever I am on the verge of solving one of the most perplexing problems in the universe, like how to convert excess methane from cows into a food source, the phone always rings and I'm yanked back into the mundane. I rub my neck. I pick up the phone. "This is Mark."

"She's so cute." It's Sue. She's with the little (miniature actually) dachshund, holding it in her arms. "Oh honey, it is so cute." I can hear the puppy yipping and yapping in the background. I imagine it stretching its cute little neck—actually, one can think of a dachshund as little more than a neck with a butt and a nose—stretching up to Sue's celestial countenance and giving her an endearing, irresistible doggy lick. "She's the runt," she says. "Her name is Fergie and she's just the cutest thing you've ever seen."

I feel it deep down inside, a profound psychic surge of pure a priori knowledge percolating up from the bedrock of my existence. All my life I have wanted to own a big golden dog, a manly dog with a thick leather collar, one that I could romp with out in the meadow, a dog that would love me in a slobbery muscling way, like guys like; a dog that knocks you over with its pure, untempered affection. The knowledge that I will instead become the owner of a dog approximately the size and shape of an Italian sausage becomes so clear in my mind and heart that I feel myself actually make one of those tectonic shifts of acceptance, like the shift one makes when one realizes that one is never going to get to sleep with Mary Ann Oxley, who was our head cheerleader in high school, or share a stage with Bruce Springsteen. I hear it rising up from the depths: I'm going to own a weenie dog.

"Can I bring her home?" She says. "How much?" I inquire. "She's so little," she says. "What are we going to do with a dog, though, Honey? I mean, Sue, we haven't figured out an eating regimen for ourselves yet. It will starve here. What do they eat, anyway? What if the dog doesn't like us? Dogs have rights now you know. They have lawyers. If they don't like the home they're placed in they sue. We have to think about exposure, sweetheart?

"Oh, Honey. I'll take care of her. How much can a cute little thing like this eat?" "OK," I fire back firmly. "But you're going to feed it. Honey? Honey? Are you still there?" Sue is purring over the phone. This happens to me all the time, too. Since I'm never sure what I do or do not want from life—success in business, spiritual attainments or the new surround sound home entertainment center—my wife Sue, my beautiful, inimitable mate, who came into my life straight out of the mystical spheres themselves, has taken over and transformed my tentative posture into a firm, determined direction, basically hers. "Fine," I say. "But it's your dog. I'm not feeding the damn thing no matter how cute it is." And I think to myself, there's not a meadow within two hundred miles of here.

Since we haven't communicated much over the last two years, this Yuletide greeting might be the perfect place to thank everyone for coming to the wedding, even though we kind of forget who was there. Hey. OK. It took place over a year ago and you haven't heard a word from us since the canapé fiasco at the

Ritz Carlton, but there's a good reason for that. Sue and I had an epiphany. It was one of those once-in-a-lifetime experiences in which the clouds part and the sky opens and you shimmer inside with a sensation that is so absolute and unequivocal that you feel it must be coming from God herself. We were sitting together amidst the silent aftermath of a warm and jubilant wedding reception at the Ritz, surrounded by empty champagne bottles, lukewarm stainless steel steam tables from which the canapés had long ago disappeared, and Uncle Bob, who was still resting his head in the flower bed. We were sitting together on a round settee holding hands and staring deeply into one another's eyes, when suddenly it dawned on us, "Do you feel it?" I asked. Overwhelmed by the intensity of the sensation, Sue nodded her head. We smiled, utterly entranced, utterly in love. And I said, "We're married." She nodded and tears began to appear on her cheeks. I held her tight in my arms and said, "This means we can have sex any time we want, doesn't it?" She sobbed and nodded.

Today, Sue and I have what I would call the ideal spousal relationship. I'm not saying that we don't have problems. Sue's not perfect. One thing, for example, is she only eats what she needs. I don't know what that is all about, but it always makes me a little uneasy. How would you feel if your dinner partner, with a delicate, aristocratic gesture, was raising a perfectly formed snow pea to her mouth, while you, on the opposite side of the table, were finding out how much pork sausage and gravy you could fit on your fork? Second, she's very superficial, in the literal sense of the word. That is, if the surface, like kitchen counters and floors and desktops and stuff, look clean and spiffy, then from Sue's point of view, they are spiffy. It doesn't matter if underneath and behind the surface the drawers and cabinets look like the streets of Calcutta. And those sandals! Sometimes she walks around in shiny gold sandals that look like they're made out of drapes from Versailles. Just as I am ready to make a major breakthrough in my cosmology, Sue walks by in those gold sandals, FLIP FLOP FLIP FLOP FLIP FLOP! And I totally lose my new contribution to the Unified Field Theory.

She doesn't make it easy, but with my anger management class going so well, and with our epiphanies still fresh in our minds, Sue and I are seeing a pretty good future ahead. Minor things notwithstanding (whatever that means), we both feel we have entered into a warm, wonderful, and nurturing relationship. It's like Samuel Beckett used to say, ordinary love lived day-to-day becomes extraordinary.

Ok! It happened again: Just as I was getting ready to jot down a new algorithm that would have helped the people at JPL get to Mars, the front door bursts open and Sue walks in with a big solar smile on her face and one of those portable doggy cages in her hand. "We're home," she says. I spasm back to reality. She sets the cage down next to my desk. I default to the human condition, get down on my hands and knees and peek inside the cage. Two big brown eyes, sad as Bambi after the fire, peer back out at me. "She's soooo cute," I think silently to myself, while maintaining a firm grimace. The little dachshund was quivering inside like one of those machines that mix up paint in the can. I opened up the cage, and very slowly her pointed little snout emerged, sniffing a little with that nose that sees. Then her head, with tiny velvet ears the color of rich walnut wood. Then one front foot. Then, very tentatively, the other. Then she's out. She looks at me. Her little wiener tale starts to wag. This dog is so small that I could fit it into a sock. I look up at Sue. She's looking down, with a tear in her eye. I say, "What have you done?" And she says, "There was just no way I could leave her there."

That was the end our sleep for the next month. And the end of our carpet. And the end of life as I knew it. (MIT could just forget about any help from me.) First, Fergie cried every night, outside the door of our bedroom. We had made her a nice comfortable poster bed with a down comforter and doggy wallpaper and toys and little bits and pieces from her former home to fool her into thinking she was still with her previous owner. (Her previous owners, by the way, were reprehensible Yuppies who had purchased the poor dog as a test to see if they were capable of taking care of an animal before actually having a child. Can you imagine? And then when the wife got pregnant she said, "I can't possibly take care of a dog AND a baby," and so they sold Fergie to us.) Anyway, Fergie wasn't fooled by any of the stuff we piled on top of her. She just howled ad infinitum. "Let her cry," I explained to Sue. "She's got to learn to be by herself."

At three in the morning, while sleeping on the floor in the hallway, almost inside of the dog box, I thought to myself, is this what the creation of the universe was supposed to achieve? A man, no longer young, sleeping in a dog box with a neck, a nose and butt. The next night, Sue slept in the hall, on the floor. Then me. Then Sue. The next night, I began to drink and take drugs again.

During the day, Fergie threw up. "She has a very sensitive stomach," Sue explained to me while I wiped the stringent yellow bile off the new sofa.

The vile white Yuppies who had previously owned Fergie had kept her inside of the portable cage almost all the time; that's where she lived. They were very strict disciplinarians, which meant they forbid the poor dog from ripping up their furniture, peeing on their rug or even barking. Poor little Fergie did not know how to play and she never barked. "Something is wrong with her," I pointed out to Sue. "A weenie dog that doesn't bark is like a Doberman that doesn't kill." She was definitely in need of some play therapy.

I threw one of her toys across the room, hoping she would bolt after it and fetch it back. When she sat there staring up at me like I had just spoken something in Chinese, I knew I'd have to model the behavior for her. "Honey," I said to Sue, "throw the badger (Dachshunds were bred to hunt badgers and miniature dachshunds were bred to hunt little tiny badgers, so we sewed her up a miniature badger.). I got down on my hands and knees and chased the badger across the floor, skidding to a stop in front of it, then leaning over and picking it up between my teeth. "There! You get it, Ferg?"

Gradually we got her to play with her toys, to run after them, pick them up between her teeth and shake them back and forth as if they were . . . well, badgers. Then I taught her the head game. This game came about when I realized that the dog loved to lick people's faces. Nothing made her happier than licking your face and she would go to great lengths to reach up and stick her little tongue inside your nose, ear, or mouth. So, what I did was to get down on my hands and knees again, and then lean my head way down until it butted with her own. She'd try to lick my face, of course, but I would quickly twist my head so that my face would be out of reach. Fergie would maneuver to squeeze her cone-of-a-nose between the floor and my face, but I would move again. So, we'd spend hours on the floor, Fergie trying to get a lick in, and me shifting and avoiding her moves. Every time she scored a lick, she'd get a point. If I prevented her from getting in a lick for eight seconds, I'd get a point. The winner got a bone.

So, Fergie learned to play, and eventually she learned how to bark (which she has been doing ever since). After living inside the cage for a year (which was basically for her whole life) it took her a while to figure out the possibilities that freedom presented; like licking faces, chasing fake badgers and barking at everything that moved. But once she got a taste of it, the joys of freedom were just about all she wanted, plus some meat now and then.

And that's what we'd like to wish for you this Christmas: not meat, but that you get out of your cages and discover those parts of yourself that may have been stymied by reality. That was actually one of the vows that Sue and I made when we got married, that we'd try and open up the cage as much as possible, and coax one another to come out and play, even chase a stuffed badger now and then if it felt right. There are miracles. I think the fact that you're still reading this letter is proof of that, and one of the big ones is that the human soul can be forgiven and renewed. Christmas is the time to remember that, in fact, it's the time to do it: forgive, renew, play the head game and transform the ordinary into the extraordinary. Merry Christmas.

With our miraculous love and best wishes,

Sue, Mark and Fergie

PS: We're absolutely NOT having a baby.

1988
Important Events

- **Solidarity struggles for freedom against repressive Communist regime in Poland.**

  Sue and Mark buy weenie dog.

- **Lloyd Bentsen tells Dan Quayle, " . . . you're no Jack Kennedy".**

  Sue tells Mark, "You're no Jack Kennedy, either. In fact, you're no Sergeant Schriver."

- **The head of NASA makes dire warnings about greenhouse gases.**

  Sue and Mark cut down on breathing.

- **The price of fax machines drops to just under $2000.**

  But Sue and Mark had already spent their money on the weenie dog.

The Year of Tears

Mark, Sue and Fergie
Orange County, California

December 1989

Dear Friends and Family,

Another miracle! Lara Louise was born on November 21. Won't stop crying. No sleep. Please send help.

Merry Christmas

Love,
Sue, Mark & Lara

1989
Important Events

- **The Exxon Valdez runs aground in Prince William Sound.**

  Damage to the sound NOTHING compared to what weenie dog did to carpet.

- **Oat bran was big diet fad.**

  Mark sprinkles oat bran over his Hagen Daz.

- **Field of Dreams comes out and Pete Rose gets caught betting on baseball.**

  Sue tells Mark, "You're no Kevin Costner."

- **Democracy movement in Tianamen Square is crushed by Red Chinese troops.**

  Mark buys "Remember Tianamen Square" bumper sticker. Sue buys one that says, "Free Zsa Zsa."

- **Dow Jones closes at a record 2734.**

  Mark explains to Sue, "It's too high. Never buy when it's high."

- **The Berlin Wall comes down and the world is free of communism.**

  Lara Louise Mendizza is born.

The Sleepless Years

Mark, Sue, Lara and Fergie
Orange County, California

Christmas 1990

Dear Friends and Family,

Huh? Hello? Where am I? What? Geeez! I feel like I just woke up from a weird dream. It was Christmas Eve and I was—and this was the really scary part—a parent. Wait a minute! My God! I am a parent. Ahhhhhhhh!

OK. Have you noticed anything strange about this baby thing? I mean have you noticed they don't ever leave? They're like little tiny guests who come for a visit, have some breast milk, and then just stay, like forever. That was nowhere in the books I read.

Lara came to visit last year and, sure enough, she's still here! She turned one on November 21, so I guess it's pretty obvious what Sue and I have been doing. I believe "parenting" is the word they use. But "staying-awake-forever" would be a better verb. Except for the shuteye we get in traffic on the 405 freeway (an acquired skill here in Southern California), Sue and I haven't slept for a year. We go to bed. Get up. Go to bed. Get up. Go to bed. Get up. The Chinese used this technique to get spies to tell them their secrets. And it works. We would have told for sure, plus turned in our parents: "Here's their address. They're home.

Yes, they're spies. Take 'em. Just let us sleep." There were times last February when we actually started looking around for the receipt the birthing center gave us after we paid our bill. "What was the return policy on that deal," I asked Sue, over the eternal din of our precious wailing daughter. But you can never find those papers when you need them, and so we decided to keep her—Lara Louise—and she has unfolded before us like a whimsical, mysterious flower while we—Sue and I—have become her slaves.

The birth itself was pretty awesome because we (I was there, too) did it au-natural as they say. No doctors. No anesthesia. No episiotomy or pain medication whatsoever, and believe me I could have used a little something. It all started after we read these books that told us babies; nay, not babies, but fetuses in that prenatal state during which they resemble something between a starchild and a gecko, are soulful creatures responding to every thought and action that the mother and her surroundings – I was considered a "surrounding"– afforded. According to prenatalists, nothing slips by these little whatevers. They hear every word; they feel all your emotions; they're reading your mind all the time. And they don't like educated people, especially doctors. If you don't want your child to turn out like Saddam Hussein, they say, then you can't smoke or drink or think impure thoughts, and you have to deliver your baby in the kitchen sink.

Since Sue and I knew nothing about babies, and had a pretty high gullibility rating, this all sounded plausible. So we hired a midwife. Allison was born and raised in the West Indies and received her training at Midwife University in London. She is a large, black, born-again Christian woman with big lanolin hands, which had spent more time in-utero than any human being ever, and had delivered more babies than Welby and Kildare combined. Allison operates a birthing center in Anaheim. It has little rooms decorated by Laura Ashley, and storks can be seen daily launching themselves gracefully off the rooftop. What we liked more than her belief in the Lord and her long list of testimonials was her absolute confidence in the birth process. "With the Lord's help," she would say, "woman have been delivering babies for over three million years and most of that time without the benefit of anesthesia and large metal utensils." I swear to God, Allison was so full of faith and exuberance that she could have reached in and pulled a baby out of me if she'd wanted to.

You gotta try this! I mean you gotta have a baby, just to see what it's like; because it is unlike anything else in the whole world. And I didn't even have it. Sue had it. I mean her. I mean Sue had her, Lara. Do you want to hear about this? Want to hear about "our" labor. I know it sounds like a cliché, but this event was so profound, so holy and bloody and volcanic that it's hard to get your arms around it. After downing a glass of prune juice and castor oil, which Allison had prescribed over the phone as a natural inducement, Sue had been in labor for about five hours. Allison was on the floor reaching into Sue's body with her big intuitive hands and asking with murmured but passionate prayer for help from Jesus. Sue's body was in continuous convulsions. I was supporting her and her back pressed into my chest with a force that bordered on the supernatural. She was possessed, her body not her own, but a fierce momentous spasm with a purpose so singular that it cut through all human pretense and convention. I mean nobody is cool during childbirth. Breathe, I said softly. Push, I screamed. Sue was in another world altogether, and I cannot begin to imagine it. She was soaked with perspiration, deep in birthing trance and maybe just a little pissed off at me for being a man. The baby's head, Lara's head, was midway through the cervix. Sue seemed to lack the strength for the final push necessary to place Lara into the world, and Allison was worried that if it did not pass very soon there was a chance the child would be hurt. "Sue," she said with unequivocal urgency. "If you do not give birth to this baby very soon I am going to take you to the hospital and perform a Cesarean." Then she closed her eyes and prayed. Sue pushed like Samson, like the crowd on the first day of Nordstrom's After-Thanksgiving Day Sale, like Zena herself she pushed and Lara Louise somewhat reluctantly came forth. She was beautiful. She looked around slowly, god-like in a way, if a little bewildered, and I could tell that she recognized us immediately. I could even tell what she was thinking: You guys! You two are going to be my parents?

A few hours later we were in the car driving home, Lara swaddled snuggly in the car seat; Sue in a catatonic daze. We later understood why women go to hospitals to deliver their babies. It's not because they need all that equipment. It can all be done in the sink. It's for the rest, the badly needed sleep and recuperation that a woman needs after the baby is born. Sue didn't get any of that at home and we decided that a better idea would have been to have the baby in the bathtub, and then go to the hospital for a few days. Anyway, we were all pretty dazed driving home on the five freeway, each in our own way trying to fathom what had just happened and perhaps more urgently, what was to come. We carried Lara into the house, and guess who met us! Fergie looked up at Lara, and Lara looked down at Fergie, and then Lara started to cry. It's been a year, and she hasn't stopped.

Here's how it went: At four o'clock each afternoon our little angel began to cry, and she doesn't stop until about one o'clock in the morning. Sue holds her in her arms, rocking her back and forth hour after hour and talking to her, always talking to her, and even though Lara is wailing at a pretty good decibel level,

Sue hears none of that. She holds her close and hears only Lara's little soul speaking to her intimately from way down deep in the universe about how thoroughly bound together they are in love. Sue rocks and cuddles, while I watch. That's what fathers do mostly, we watch and stand ready to run to the drug store. Plus, we go invisible.

This is something they don't tell you about in those big parenting books that are so thick you can use them as furniture. It's true. After the birth of a child, fathers become totally transparent, virtually nonexistent beings. Here's an example. The doorbell rings. I open it and three of Sue's women friends are there to visit the mother and child. How lovely, I think to myself. I greet them cordially, "Hi Gladys, Karen, Julie." But they don't say anything. They just walk right through me to the bedroom where Sue and Lara are cooing; not past or around or over me, but straight through me, with their little rattles and blankets and books by Beatrice Potter. It was like I wasn't even there. Which I guess I wasn't. In fact, I was invisible pretty much all last year, except of course when there was a need for more Desitin and Pedialite.

At eleven o'clock Lara is still crying and it's my turn to take over. I bundle her up and put her into the car seat of the big blue Volvo we bought, "because it's a good solid car for kids." Then I drive around, rather aimlessly. It's the only thing that has been effective in getting Lara to sleep. The drone of the car I think, and maybe the movement; I don't know. Nobody knows. It shocked me at first. I kept saying, "You mean we can put the Hubble Telescope into orbit and describe the origins of the universe, but we can't help a kid to fart?" Nope, said the doctors. Don't know, said the specialists. Just happens that way, said the great pediatric minds of the world. But everybody else had a recommendation: "Let her cry." "She's not getting enough to eat. Add some formula to your breastfeeding." "Put a little whiskey into the formula." "She needs a routine." "Feed her later." Put the vacuum cleaner next to her crib and turn it on." "Try a bath." "Try incense." "Try Beano." We tried everything. Nothing worked but driving around the Southland at night. I would move my hand over to Lara's and extend my pointer finger. She would hold on to it as we drove and occasionally give me a little smile, which was probably a gas reaction, and we would drive south, listening to lullabies in the Volvo, in the starlight, on the way to Mexico, quietly and happily falling asleep.

I know this isn't much of a Christmas Letter, but it's all I can do right now. It's late. I've got to wrap presents and then Lara and I have to hit the road. May you all "sleep in heavenly peace" as the song goes.

Till next year,
With our weary love,

Sue, Lara, Fergie & The Invisible Man

1990
Important Events

- **Manuel Noriega surrenders to U.S. officials.**
  Sue and Mark offer to switch places with Noriega, if he takes care of the baby.

- **New England Journal of Medicine reports that oat bran does NOT play a role in significantly reducing cholesterol.**
  Mark goes back to pouring scotch over his Hagen Daz.

- **Real Estate values drop sharply.**
  Who cares? Baby has gas!

- **S & L bailout costs American taxpayers $182 billion.**
  Which is nothing compared to what Mark and Sue have spent on disposable diapers.

- **Question for the world is "Who killed Laura Palmer?"**
  Question for Sue and Mark is, "Where is Lara Mendizza?"
  "I thought YOU had her!"

- **Lech Walesa becomes president of Poland.**
  Lara turns one. Weenie dog is two.

Mark, Sue, Lara and Fergie
Orange County, California

Christmas 1991

Dear Friends and Family,

Yes, we're two! I mean Lara is two. I mean we made it to two. I mean we only have sixteen more years of parenting. It is arduous, but the moments of life that slip in between the parenting are precious and I'm sure they are the reason the human race has been doing timeouts and stuff for three million years. Lara is still the sun around which our lives are orbiting, but we have managed to add a few things to our lifestyle this year, like we went to a movie in September. Sue hated it. "From now on I choose the films," she said, and I think, ouch! Audrey Hepburn. Sue quickly reads my mind and says, "Well, you'll never see Audrey Hepburn drive her convertible over a cliff."

With Lara maturing and the Soviet Union dissembling, I think we all got a little more sleep in 1991. I wrote scripts, and learned how to crawl on the floor. Sue left the high school and has been teaching German, Spanish and English at the local community college. In our spare time, we compare our child with all the other two- and three-year olds in the neighborhood. "Smarter than Tiffany, don't you think?" "Oh, yea, way smarter."

In April, Sue and I attended a self-improvement workshop

in San Jose. The techniques we were taught were extremely effective as long as we remained inside the workshop, but once we walked out onto the street and missed the shuttle to the airport, we slipped right back into our unimproved state. While we were in San Jose, Sue's mom, Edna, was taking care of Lara. When we returned home, they were both in the garage, and we knew instantly that something was wrong. Lara could not breathe. Her little breaths were short and labored and sounded like a percolating coffee pot. We rushed her to the emergency room where the doctor examined her and immediately understood the problem, "Asthma," he said. Asthma? What do you mean Asthma? I don't believe it. She doesn't have Asthma. What is asthma, anyway? And we spent the rest of the year finding out. The condition. The diagnosis. The treatment. The drugs. The steroids. The awfulness of asthma. I don't want to go into it here in a Christmas letter, but it turned out to be true: Lara has Asthma, and it just . . . well, knocked the breath out of us.

But we got used to that, too; just like we got used to sleeping on the freeway, changing diapers in the parking lot and feeling the angels descend into our home as we held our child in our arms.

Unfortunately, our precious child learned to whine this year, which the specialists say is an indication that she is becoming an adult much sooner than expected. She's singing songs, too. But the biggest developmental change I think is that she's begun to remember things. Boy, does that change the parenting equation. We used to be able to pacify her with a tender remark, a rattle or an empty promise. But no more. Now she REMEMBERS. It ushers in a whole new set of parenting strategies known as lying.

This is also the first year that Lara has embraced the idea of Santa Claus. It's an almost psychedelic concept: a funny old man in a red suit and white beard who flies through the air in a magic sled drawn by eight spirited reindeer, a merry old soul who slides down the chimney at night when everyone is sleeping and places gifts for the kids under the Christmas tree.

"Sounds good to me," says Lara, and she goes "ho-ho-ho" whenever she hears his name.

When I asked Lara what she would like Santa Claus to bring to her, she hesitated for a moment and thought, or at least it looked like thinking to me. Then she said, "Presents." "But what kind of presents?" I asked. And here's what I found interesting. Lara thought some more. Her face strained a little with intense two-year-old concentration, eyes moving up to the left, and then over to the other side. Her little brow drew toward the center, but nothing seemed to come to mind. Either she didn't understand the question, or she just hadn't reached the point in her development where she could imagine a desire that wasn't already ripe and fulfilled in her present moment. I mean she has never had any trouble saying things like "I want that!" or the contracted version which is used in conjunction with a finger point, "THAT!" So, I tried to coax her a little. "Would you like him to bring you a truck?" I asked. She instantly said, "Yes!" "Would you like Santa to bring you a new house?" "Yes!" she said with executive certainty. "Would you like a new dress?" "Yes!" she nodded. And then I asked again, "Well, what else would you like for Santa to bring to you?" Lara slipped back into that thoughtful state again and seemed to be searching for the meaning of the question as much as for the answer. I waited. She thought and thought and thought, and finally she came up with an answer. "A

NEW present," she said with a great deal of satisfaction. "A NEW present?" I repeated. And she was sure this time, "Yes, a "NEW" present."

Not a truck or a house or dress, but a NEW present. I thought that made a lot of sense. Instead of trying to think up a long list of things that we would like Santa Claus to bring us, maybe it would be better if we left it a little more abstract this time and go with what Santa and his elves think we would be happiest with: a new car for the family? Yes! A new diamond ring for our finger? Yes! A big new balance in our checkbook? Oh yeah, Santa! Or maybe a new friend, or a new thought, a new world, perhaps, or a fresh new way of beholding the one that surrounds us. That's what we're wishing for everyone this Christmas and for ourselves too. It doesn't really matter what Santa brings, as long as it's new, as long as you make it NEW.

So that's our wish for you this year: A Merry Christmas and Happy New Year to all, and to all a bunch of "NEW."

With our love,

Mark, Fergie, Sue and Lara

1991
Important Events

- **Desert Storm begins, January 16th.**

  Lara learns to whine.

- **Rodney King videotape is played for weeks and weeks.**

  Lara discovers the concept of Santa Claus.

- **Dow hits 3000**

  Mark explains to Sue "Way to high! No way we're buying at these prices."

- **Americans discover "lattes."**

  Lara begins to remember things, forcing Sue and Mark to lie about stuff.

- **Boris Yeltsin becomes first elected president of the Russian Republic.**

  Sue tells Mark, " . . . you're no Boris Yeltsin."

- **President Gorbachev resigns and Soviet Union dissolves.**

  Lara learns how to say, "HO – HO – HO.

Mark, Sue, Lara and Fergie
Orange County, California

Christmas 1992

Dear Friends and Family,

Don't you just hate those Christmas notes you get every year in which parents, usually new parents, dwell on the perceived accomplishments of their offspring? They go something like this:

"Merry Christmas. Although Heather just turned three months, she's already reading at the 6-month reading level, which is way above grade level."

"Wade, the prankster, is doing well too. He turned five this year and just yesterday he switched our toothpaste for a tube of Heather's Desitin, which we both used to brush our teeth. We've decided to trade Wade in for a Trevor."

They go on to tell you that after Heather completes her dancing career with the American Ballet Theater, she plans to help Stephen Hawking reconcile Einstein's General Theory of Relativity with Quantum Mechanics. The older son, Taylor, who is thirty-two, they tell you with a proud glow, has finally decided what he wants to be in life: an actor. "He looks just like Tom Cruise," they beam.

Fortunately for you, Sue and I are not like those parents. Sure, Lara turned three in November and she's already handling our investment portfolio and likes to tease the other kids with little aphorisms from Frederick Nietzsche's *Ecco Homo*. She's more beautiful than Heather will ever be, but we know how tedious and boring those "prodigy" letters can be and we've decided to strike a slightly higher note this year and stick to a pithier subject matter: like my bad back, for example, and Sue's TMJ operation.

It's true! Sue had an operation on her jaw. Ever since the table fell on her head at work back in 1990—which could explain a lot of things—she's had real problems with her jaw. Worker's Comp finally authorized corrective surgery and Sue went in about a week ago.

I, of course, was the one that suffered the most. First of all, while Sue was in the operating room sleeping, I had to wait out in the lobby for 12 hours reading old issues of Omni magazine, and anxiously pondering the fate of the nation as it finally dawned upon me that America had turned over her nuclear arsenals to someone about my age and, more frightening than that, to someone who had no doubt read a lot of the same books I had during his formative years. Like, "*The Yaqui Way with Intercontinental Ballistic Missiles,*" if you know what I mean. Then, when they finally allowed me to see her in the recovery room, I felt compelled to lecture the doctors and nurses on how best to care for her. "Hey, what's this tube doing in her arm?" I said. "Somebody forgot to take out the tube."

Fortunately, Sue was still under the anesthesia and didn't have to witness my intervention. She says she had the best rest she's had in three years and she's organizing another surgery soon, just to get another night's sleep, still a luxury in our household due to Lara's limitless energy resources.

For example, at 10 o'clock at night after Sue and I have read "When You Give a Moose a Muffin" three times and "When You Give a Mouse a Cookie" four times and "The Cat in the Hat" twice and when we're both rapidly sliding down the slippery slope of parental fatigue into a delirious catatonic state, Lara bursts out with her two favorite phrases: "ONE MORE TIME!" and "I WANT SOME MILK!" Three years into the blissful mysteries of parenthood and sleep is still a dream.

But we're not talking about Lara this year 'cause we need room for my lumbar spine. It's much better, actually. We had a pretty bad bout back in July—I say "we" because when I am suffering I make a point of making sure that everyone else is suffering too: "Can somebody just please get me the remote control please. I mean what do you expect me to do, get up from the couch all by myself with this terrrrrrrrible PAIN IN MY BACK?" It's not a pretty sight. But you'll all be pleased to hear that the inflammation is down and as long as I watch my posture and take lots of breaks from my time at the word processor, the doctor says I have a chance of living an almost normal life. Of course, my doctor doesn't know Lara very well. He still throws out the concept of "normal" as if it exists in the real world.

He doesn't know, for example, how much Lara loves to be thrown up into the air and then caught as she sails back down to earth like an egret across a placid mountain lake. The big difference here, of course, is that egrets have wings. I toss her up to the ceiling. The fourth, fifth and sixth discs in the L-spine pop like plastic bubble packing material when you pinch it between your fingers. She squeals with glee and I really love it, too. Then she comes back down and I catch her like one of the great Zambisi brothers. Another millimeter of cartilage grinds off and finds its way down the spinal cord. But I ask you, what are backs for if not to teach our children that they are perfectly capable of flying through the air like an egret? What, ultimately, are we here for if not to give our lives—backs, sleep and all—to our children? At least that's how Lara sees it.

Which brings us to our little Christmas greeting. Here's what happened last night, the night before, and every night for about the last two and half years. First, Sue and I put Lara to sleep in her bed and the two of us retired to ours. About one o'clock in the morning, Lara woke up and yelled to us across the hallway, "Can I come into your bed?" After having read all those twelve inch thick early childhood development books, most of which are devoted to carefully worded warnings which state, never, absolutely never allow your child to crawl into bed with you, we said, "OK!"

Lara walked in sleepily with her doll under her arm and climbed in with us. But she was a little restless. She wanted to tell us about the chicken noodle soup that she found in her bath water. Sue always spends an hour or so listening and comforting Lara, but I gotta get up early, so I climbed out of our bed and go into Lara's room where I climbed into hers. I pull the *Beauty and the Beast* comforter up to my chin and went to sleep with the beast staring deeply into my eyes.

Lara flails around when she sleeps, so about five o'clock, Sue sneaked into Lara's room too and climbed into bed with me. At five oh seven, Lara woke up and discovered that she was sleeping in mommy's and daddy's bed— ALONE. I've been betrayed! She got up and started looking for the traitors. We hid. We pulled the *Beauty and the Beast* comforter over our heads and didn't say a word. She found us and we all laughed and right after Lara climbed under the covers with Sue and me, Fergie, the killer dachshund, discovered that she too had been abandoned and jumped into the *Beauty and the Beast* comforter with her three humans.

So, there we were, me, Sue, Lara and Fergie lying together at five in the morning in Lara's single bed. I asked Lara what she wanted for Christmas. She told us she wants a blue basketball. "Done!" I said, somewhat relieved. Sue started to fall back to sleep. I reached over and tickled her for fun and Lara instinctively came to her rescue. "Don't you hurt my mommy," she said to me with stern, playful eyes. Then she slid her hand around mommy's neck in an affectionate, protective way. She looked at Sue and said, "Mommy, I'll take care of you." A pause. A moment later, she turned her head and looked at me and a second thought occurred to her. She slid her arm around my neck in an equally protective manner and she said, "Daddy, I'll take care of you, too." And then she hugged the two of us and our heads bumped together like the Three Stooges.

That's our Christmas wish this year: that you feel and know in your hearts and minds that no matter how unlikely it may seem to you sometimes—like when riots are happening across town—we're all being taken care of and, eventually, we'll all receive the blue basketballs of our dreams.

Have a very Merry Christmas, Hanukkah, Ramadan, Kwanzaa etc. and please write to us and let us know how your cosmetic surgeries are working for you.

With Much Protection & Love,

Sue, Mark, Lara & Fergie

1992
Important Events

- **The word "Not" becomes hot.**

  As in, "I'm glad you're not John Kennedy . . . NOT!"

- **12-year-old Gregory Kingsley sues to sever parental rights with his natural mother, and wins.**

  Sue and Mark tell Lara sure, you can sleep in our bed. But NOT your lawyer.

- **Bill Clinton elected the 42nd president of the U.S.**

  Lara wants a blue basketball for Christmas.

- **Ross Perot refers to a large black NAACP audience as "you people."**

  Sue and Mark introduce Lara to a black person.

- **Prince Charles and Diana separate.**

  Mark and Sue stop talking about the royal family in front of child.

- **People swoon over the book, "The Bridges of Madison County".**

  Sue and Mark break world record for number of times reading "When You Give a Mouse a Cookie" out loud.

The Year of Flames

Mark, Sue, Lara and Fergie
Orange County, California

Christmas 1993

Dear Friends and Significant Others,

Hey! Christmas again. Another trip around the sun. Another year of carefree living out here in Southern California where the mountains meet the sea, 200,000 aerospace workers meet at the unemployment office and the flames from hell meet Laguna Beach and Malibu. Oh yeah, I forgot: the Menendez brothers had a meeting with their mom and dad, and Damian Williams met up with Reginald Denny. Clearly, a year of remarkable meetings. And we've still got Michael Jackson to get through.

It doesn't sound so good if you listen to the news, so we don't. We're too busy being totally happy. We didn't even know the equity in our house had dropped by 10% until our loan guy broke into hysterical laughter while reviewing our refi app. Didn't even phase us, though. We've been reading these self-help books lately, so nothing gets to us. The books tell us that nothing that happens to you is really real; it's what you make of it; it's how you respond to things, not the things themselves that makes up your personal reality, and they tell us that we're in complete control of our own individual responses. So, in a way, they say, we create our own reality. Cool!

I was explaining this whole idea to Sue back in October when we looked out the window and saw this enormous pall of black smoke billowing over the foothills behind our house. Altadena had burned the day before. Laguna Beach was, at the time, in flames. And now it looked like we were going to burn, too. But, hey! We're in charge, right? I scanned the index of our self-help book to see how best to respond to this particular reality, but by the time I got to "inferno," Sue was pulling the family photos out from under the bed and taking the oils off the wall. "What are you doing?" I ask. "Taking charge of my reality," she responds. "Getting out of here."

Like most other residents of Southern California during the fires, I got out the camera and started taking photos of all our personal belongings to prove to the insurance company that our kitchen table was actually an Italian antique from the seventeenth century. "Hey, don't forget the Renoir," I say to Sue.

Evacuation was a new concept for Lara, but she took to it like she does everything else: with absolute abandon and enthusiasm. She began a pile of all the things she wanted to take with her: five puzzles, a pair of pajama bottoms, one Birkenstock, a cast figure of Beauty and the Beast, about thirty books, some yarn, a cup, lots of socks and of course her yellow umbrella.

Lara's been around the sun about four times now and for each trip she takes it seems like Sue and I take about five. Lara becomes more beautiful, articulate, bright and unpredictable. Sue and I become, like: posthumous. Lara is sort of at that contrary stage where no matter what you ask her to do she'll always respond by wanting to do the opposite. Us: "Let's go to school, honey." Lara: "I don't want to go to school." Us: "No, sweetheart. There's no school today." Lara: "But I miss my friends. I want to go to school." So whenever we want something from her we just ask for its opposite. Us: "Let's don't eat our peas tonight, OK?" Lara: "No, I want to eat my peas."

I say she's unpredictable because four-year-olds come up with some really mysterious thoughts and expressions. We were driving down the street the other day and I said to Lara, "You know honey, you're my best friend. I always know what you're thinking and you always know what I'm thinking. She turned and said, "Yes. And you always know what I'm dreaming and I always know what you're dreaming." Now, where did that come from, I wonder? And then I thought, hope it's not true!

Lara got the chicken pox this year and Job himself could not have suffered more. We spent about four days in a bathtub filled with oatmeal and then another two days with that pink calamine lotion spread all over the house. After it was over, we just painted the house pink to match the spots on the walls.

Of course, neither Sue nor I have had a full night's sleep since Lara joined the family. To get rest, Sue schedules TMJ operations and sleeps in the recovery room. I sleep at meetings and conferences and on the 405 freeway. But it's been worth it, right? Right?

And Sue's career has really taken some interesting turns. Since joining the staff at Rancho Santiago Community College, she's gone from teaching to developing educational programs for the Department of Social Services, or what some people call Jail. Yes, JAIL. She's doing time. "You're makin' us look bad," said the judge. "Maybe a little jail time will teach you the value of crude and repulsive behavior, which happens to be a fundamental value of our society."

I'm kidding. Sue's in charge of the college's Inmate Education Program for the Orange County Jail. Can you believe it? Sue, who makes Mary Poppins look like Cruella deVil, is in charge of teaching parenting and computer skills to inmates whose crimes consisted not of being gangbangers or killing innocent people, but mostly of being brown with weed. I don't think Sue has ever had a more satisfying job than helping those inmates get into Harvard.

We're also compiling a book this year. It's called "You Know It's Going to Be a Good Day When . . ." And we definitely need your input. Here's the idea:

You know it's going to be a good day when. . .

- ✓You get inside the grocery store before the Girl Scouts see you.
- ✓Your kids say they're going to play at the neighbor's house.
- ✓Your saran wrap comes off the roll without shrink-wrapping your hand.
- ✓There's nothing about Bosnia Herzegovina in the newspaper.
- ✓You receive a magazine and Demi Moore is not on the cover.
- ✓You reach for the toilet paper and the roll is empty. No one's home to help. Then you discover the Kleenex box on the shelf behind you.

(Whew! Definitely going to be a good day.)

Please give the topic a little thought and send us your favorite good-day indicators.

OK, OK, I know. It's late. If you wanted to read, you would have bought a "real" book. But I want to tell you about the miracles. This is, after all, Christmas, and Christmas is nothing if not about miracles. (See: Virgin Birth). At our house, we have miracles every day. Just getting up seems to defy the laws of physics. Then there's the hair: I still have a few hairs on my head after five years of middle-aged parenting. They are few enough to count, but they're hairs nonetheless and they're still up there which is almost as remarkable as feeding the masses with a couple of trout or forgiving the entire human race for being jerks (see: History of Humanity). Another miracle is my friend Raphael.

I met Raphael while I was working in Saudi Arabia to ensure the uninterrupted flow of oil to the free world. He is one of many sons born to one of several wives of a Dinka clan leader in a southern province of the Sudan in Sub-Saharan Africa. That makes him an aristocrat. Raphael is a lawyer, too. He speaks many languages including English, Arabic, and of course, Dinka. He knows the Bible and the Koran like you know the NBA. He's black, blackest guy I know, and one of the finest people I have ever met. To make a long story short, the people in the northern part of the country killed Raphael's brother for political reasons, and they were getting ready to kill him, too. So, he escaped to Saudi Arabia and became a teacher at a school of which I was in charge. He taught English to young Saudi men so they could read the technical manuals they needed to operate the refineries that enabled oil to be exported to America which allowed us to fill up our tanks at $1.40 a gallon and drive our kids to school. Raphael's goal was to attend a university in the United States and then work through academic, political or diplomatic channels to bring peace to his country and food to his people. A U.S. degree would provide him with the respect and credibility he needed to further this goal.

While I was there, I helped him apply to Columbia, Temple, Yale, Berkeley, this one and that one. Year after year we applied. Sometimes we couldn't get transcripts from the University of Khartoum where he received his law degree. Sometimes the mail from the Middle East to the States never got where it was supposed to go. And sometimes he was simply rejected.

With peace virtually assured, I left the Middle East in 1985 and started my company here in the States. But we kept applying. Raphael got married. He began a family. He kept teaching English, which can be a thankless job for a black Christian in an Arab country. And he kept applying. Several more years passed. He was there breathing the smoke from the fires that Saddam Hussein set in the Kuwaiti oil fields. He was still there after the U.S. troops came home, still teaching, still applying.

In June I got a call from Saudi Arabia. Raphael had been accepted and granted a full three-year scholarship. Not to Columbia or Yale or Berkeley, but to Harvard University. I bet the people who wanted to kill him were really pissed off at that. He's living in Cambridge now, with his wife, his two daughters and his son. Last time I talked with him he was studying with Billy Graham at the Harvard School of Theology. To this day I'm not sure exactly how he got in. But I'm sure it was a miracle. Just as sure as I am of the hair on my head. The moral of this letter then, is: Things may never be as good as the self-help books say they're going to be, but they're never as bad as they appear on the network news, either. There's a bunch of miracles going on all the time. All we have to do is "believe," never give up, and just keep on applying.

May God Bless us All with a Merry Christmas, a Happy Hanukkah, a Cool No Rus, a Grateful Ramadan, a Hot Kwanzaa and . . . I forget the rest.

May God Just Bless the Hell Out of Us All.

Mark, Sue, Fergie & Lara

P.S. The fires were over by Halloween, but we didn't get all our stuff back on the walls and under the bed 'til Thanksgiving.

1993
Important Events

- **Southern California erupts in flames.**

  Lara learns to play the "evacuation" game.

- **The word "like" enters popular vocabulary.**

  Like when people say like the fires like burned Laguna Beach and like Malibu.

- **FBI lays siege to Branch Davidians in Waco, Texas.**

  Lara finds Easter egg hidden in her shoe.

- **President Clinton names Ruth Bader Ginsburg to Supreme Court.**

  Sue and Mark administer LSAT practice tests to Lara.

- **After 156 years as a British colony, Chinese take over rule of Hong Kong.**

  Lara gets Chicken Pox.

- **Crew of space shuttle Endeavor repairs Hubble Space Telescope in orbit.**

  Mark successfully sets clock on microwave.

The Year of Forgiveness

Mark, Sue, Lara and Fergie
Orange County, California

December 15, 1994

Dear Friends, Family and Fellow Tenured Professors,

This year cannot be over. It cannot be December already. Something must be happening to time itself. The one thing we have all grown accustomed to, that we have all come graciously to agree upon when we can hardly agree upon anything else is time, duration. And now it's changed. It has undergone some kind of weird modulation and in the process has shrunk. An hour is no longer an hour. It's about forty minutes. And a minute? Have you measured a minute, lately? More like forty seconds. Is it just me? Or do you feel it, too: the gradual shortening of durations that are so fundamental to our plans and dreams? I mean doesn't it feel like we just took down the Christmas lights a month or so ago and that 30-year fixed rates were at six percent like last week? Or maybe I'm wrong. Maybe time hasn't shortened. Maybe we just skipped something altogether this year, like summer. Did we have summer? I can't remember. Yes, that must be it. No summer. That's why it seems like such a short year. Instead of summer, we had O.J.

O.J. must be the one responsible for shortening the year. But it's not really his fault. If it weren't O.J. it would have been something else. After all, Southern California has always been a place fanatically committed to forever outdoing itself, even if it means scrapping a season or two. Last year, for example, we had to stop everything for the Michael Jackson affair and the great fires. The year before, we all stopped working to watch Rodney King and the urban riots. We lost May and June. This year, a little nervous about losing our place on the front pages of tabloids and world press alike, we offered up Nicole and Ron and O.J., and then, just to make sure nobody forgets how far ahead of the rest of the country we really are, we have Orange County go bankrupt before your very eyes. Is that cool, or what? I mean admit it, no matter where you live, no matter what municipality picks up your trash, you were all on the phone checking your derivatives, right? You know I am. We went bankrupt before any of your city fathers even thought of the idea. Now watch. Everybody's going to be doing it. God I love Southern California.

What we've started to do out here is squeeze our lives in between the great media events. After the earthquake, we do some work, have our babies, get tires for the car and stuff like that. Then, knowing for sure that something really huge is coming down the pipe, though we're not sure what, we all stock up on those little cans of disaster foods and settle down to prepare for the next big wave of epic happenings. Remember the World Cup games? That was like an epic thing. And it all happened right here. Not too many people watched the games, of course; at least not in the States. But hey, we did focus groups. We knew months ahead of time that you weren't going to watch a team that could never in its wildest dreams attain a score much above three. Forget it, right? We're a country of double-digit sport fans. It's just too hard to justify getting drunk and puking up the pepperoni pizza for a team with an average score of two. But we knew that.

We were prepared. We only put on the World Cup games for countries like Bangladesh and Yemen, underdeveloped countries whose major wars aren't as big as our pre-season games and who won't really appreciate the need for big, double-digit scoring until all the free-trade agreements kick in full speed. For us, for the event-savvy people of Southern California, the World Cup was just an excuse to promote the next big life-stopping mega-spectacle of the year.

That's right: The Three Tenors! Domingo, Carreras and Pavarotti at the L.A. Coliseum. That was the real reason for the World Cup. Tell the truth now. Didn't you get more of a thrill out of watching Carreras reach up on his tip toes and practically castrate himself right there on stage to make that high C at the end of "Nessun Dorma" than you did from watching Belgium play the Netherlands? We even thought it was better than Yanni.

So our lives in SoCal are sort of squeezed in between these major events and recurring tectonic catastrophes. Once we got Carreras back down on the ground and Pavarotti maneuvered off the stage and all the polite Italian soccer players on the plane for Rome, we started up our lives again, knowing it wouldn't be long before the next big thing usurped yet another chunk of our year.

Have you ever watched a four-year-old fall in love? It's weird. On the other hand, it's weird to watch all common sense and intelligence degrade to a pulsating mush in a twenty-, thirty- or forty-year-old, too. But the "Natal Attraction" of five is especially amusing. Lara fell in love for the first time I think in spring. Three- and four-year-old guys had fallen in love with her before, but this was the first time she'd fallen overboard. I swear, she swooned like a valley girl at the mention of little Jason's name. I mean we needed Skittles to revive her. While she and I were reading *Curious George at the Airport* (for the hundredth time), I know she was plotting ways to steal a kiss from Jason in the pre-school playroom. The swoon was genuine. The flush. The mild obsession. Of course, she can't even remember the guy's name today. (That ever happen to you?). But back in April and May you could see the whole history of human romance rise up into her cheeks and fill her four-year-old heart and mind with the irrepressible fantasies of amour. "What's it feel like to be in love?" I asked her. "It just seems silly," she said with a wisdom way beyond her four years.

As children approach the age of five, I think they become incredibly calculating, don't you? You can almost see Lara's little mind at work sometimes, like a Pentium chip imagining in nano-seconds an infinite number of consequences to a particular act or statement and trying to decide on the one that will yield unto her the greatest advantage. Sometimes she'll hold back a small percentage of the truth. She never lies, but she's very selective in what and how much she discloses. We're driving down the street, for example and she says "Daddy." I say, "What." She says, "Daddy?" I say, "What." Then she says "Daddy," one more time, and I say, "What." "Do you want me to live with you?" I think for a moment: where is this going? Is she sad? Does she think we don't want her to live with us? My mind collapses into this worried parental ball of compassion as I too run through responses and consequences. Then she says, "Daddy." I say, "What." She says, "Does Mommy want me to live with her?" And I say "Of course, honey. Mommy loves you more than anything else in the world." Now I'm really concerned. What have we done to make her feel this way? And then she says, "Well, if you buy me some of those different colored Skittles (little chewy things that cause lockjaw), then I will live with you and mommy."

Or what about this one: We're at the restaurant having breakfast together. There's a machine positioned at the entrance. It's a plastic enclosure with a miniature crane that hovers over a mountain of stuffed animals. For fifty cents you can try lowering the crane and grabbing one of the animals. "Daddy," she says. "Yes, Honey." "When we're done can we play that game?" "Have a few more bites sweetie and we'll see." "Daddy?" "Yes, honey." "How many is a few?" "Five, sweet-heart. Five is a few." "Daddy?" "Yes sweetheart." "Will you count for me because I'll be chewing and if I have to count too much I'll choke."

So now I'm counting bites. I'm forty-seven years old, a writer, a businessman, an educated, erudite, citizen of the world, and I'm counting my daughter's waffle bites at Daddy O's. It's humbling. This entire middle-aged parenting thing is such an utterly humbling endeavor. But we love it. It's the grit that creates the pearl, right? And Sue and I feel so much love for Lara and each other that we don't mind being clams—or no, I mean oysters. We don't mind being oysters. I don't think we'd want to be a clam. But being an oyster is OK.

And guess what! Back in July guess what happened! A momentous event for the Mendizza family. Give up? (That's what Lara always says, "Give up?") At precisely four and a half years old, our little Lara Louise began sleeping through the night. We couldn't believe it when it happened. This is a kid who has never taken a nap in her life, who goes to bed at nine or nine-thirty and gets up at about six or seven and who, until July 16, got up at least once and frequently two times a night, just to make sure Mommy and Daddy weren't getting any more than three hours of sleep at one time. It was killing us. We looked like Democrats after the last election. We tried everything. People used to say give it six months. Then when Lara was six months and getting up five or six times a night, they used to say a year. Give it a year. When she turned two, and was still calling out for Mommy at three in the morning, they said ignore her, just don't pay any attention to her. So, we lay there wide awake and ignored her from three to seven. When she reached four, people stopped giving us advice. They could see it in our eyes. One more suggestion to make a little bed at the foot of our own or put a little bourbon into her milk, and we would snap: During interviews after the murders people would say things like, "Sue and Mark seemed like such nice people. Not at all the kind you would imagine going through the neighborhood with an ax and a chainsaw."

This year we also reached another milestone in Sue's career. Back in May and June, before O.J. Simpson was arrested and everybody in Southern California had to stop working so they could see first-hand what kind of outfit Marsha Clarke was going to wear in court, Sue interviewed for a very important tenure-track position with the college. And she got it.

God, what a relief! Sue hates to interview. She'd rather slam her fingers in a car door or listen to Newt Gingrich lecture the Congress on the need for school prayer than sit before a group of her peers and talk about herself. We rehearsed for hours and I of course gave her some tips that I'd learned in business. "It is common to slightly stretch and perhaps even embellish one's accomplishments when faced with an extremely competitive situation," I explained. "You mean lie?" she said. "No, no, no. Did I say lie? I said embellish, highlight, push the envelope of objective truth." So, in addition to citing all her academic credentials and the long list of extraordinary achievements she's made while at the college, she also told them that she was the one that repaired the Hubbell telescope. Her work with the Pope was a big surprise to most of the people on the selection committee, too. But what cinched the deal was when she told them about her Nobel Prize. O.J. was arrested on June 17. Sue was notified of her new, tenure-track position on the 20th, just minutes before she checked into the ICU for her vacation.

Some other things happened to us this year: we saw Barbra Streisand. Bought some new Tupperware. And spent a few nights at the Ritz Carlton Hotel to celebrate our anniversary. We had gotten married at the Ritz and we've gone back every year to renew our sacred vows. We couldn't wait to get at them. We walked into our gorgeous room and swung open the French doors to reveal a spectacular full-ocean view. After being clams for so long, we felt like dolphins. We immediately sat down and, while holding hands, quietly prepared ourselves for the renewing of our sacred vows.

"You go first," Sue says to me. "No, sweetheart, why don't you go first." "I'm trying to remember the order of the vows," she says. "Yeah, the order. I forget the exact order, too. I think the first one had to do with loving one another for the rest of our lives." "Yes, and there was something about always being honest." "Yeah, yeah, love and honesty." "Did we have more than two?" "I think we said something about staying healthy all the time, working out hard at the gym and stuff like that." "We said we would TRY to stay healthy. I don't think we said we would actually stay healthy." "No you're probably right. I don't think we had a weight limit vow, or anything like that." "It's been a long time." "How long has it been anyway?" "I think about six years." "Seems like a lot longer than that. No. I didn't mean it that way, sweetheart. We didn't sleep for four and a half years. That makes it seem longer." "Call the desk. They'll remember."

We get up and call the desk. That's what we like about the Ritz. They'll do your taxes if you ask them to. They call us back after a few minutes and tell us that we were married at the hotel in November of 1987.

"Seven years (sigh)." "Yeah, seven years (sigh)." We've done a lot in seven years." "Yeah, for old people, we've done a lot." "Do you want to do the rest of our vows, now?" "To be honest, honey, I can't remember what they were." "No, me neither." "Who cares?" "Yeah, who cares? Do you love me?" "More than a hot bath." "Do you love me?" "More than a nap in the afternoon." "I think that's good enough, don't you?" "Yea, that's good enough." "Hey, look: that Cary Grant and Deborah Kerr movie is on TV." "Not Warren Beatty and Annette Benning. I don't want to see Warren Beatty and Annette Benning." "No. It's Cary Grant and Deborah Kerr." "You sure?" "Yeah." "You want to go to bed and watch it?" "Yeah."

Raphael, of course, is still studying at the Harvard School of Divinity. Last year I think I told you about what a miracle it was for him to have made the journey from the southern Sudan, to the eastern province of Saudi Arabia, to Cambridge and Harvard. The guy has been studying religion and law and world history in English, Arabic, Dinka, and now in Hebrew, too. Plus, he's right there close to the Kennedys, which gives him important insights into divinity itself. During our last phone conversation, we talked a little bit about Christianity. One of the things that makes Christianity so significant, and, in Raphael's thinking, what makes it such a clear step forward in the evolution of humankind is its emphasis on forgiveness. Sure, mercy and forgiveness are present in most other religions, but Raphael assures me that of the big three Western super-sects: Judaism, Islam, and Christianity, Jesus comes out way ahead as a teacher of forgiveness. And I think it's true. "Turn the other cheek." "Let he who has not sinned cast the first stone." "Forgive them, Father, for they know not what they do." (I use that one a lot with clients.) Before Jesus came along, most dogma taught an eye-for-an-eye sort of thing, like the Serbs and Croats have adopted in Bosnia. Think for a moment what the world would be like if we all simply forgave ourselves and our enemies. What a fresh beginning that would be. I'm not talking about forgiving the Orange County Board of Supervisors for what they did to our investment portfolio or anything crazy like that, but we could give a little slack to our other enemies, like . . . well . . . like the cable company. If you don't feel very merciful this Christmas, and it is perfectly understandable, especially if you haven't finished your shopping yet, then Raphael also had some observations about how one might bring some forgiveness and grace back into one's life. He calls it prayer. But it's not like my kind of prayer where you bow your head quietly and then plead with all your might for a new contract or a reduction in short-term interest rates. Raphael says that isn't the kind of prayer he has in mind.

Raphael: In my life, one moment of grace informs the next moment. The grace from the last moment informs the moment I am in right now. So that if I did something right a moment ago and I am about to divert into doing something wrong now, the moment ago would inform this moment that no: this is not the direction you want to take.

Mark: One continuous, seamless state of perpetual prayer.

Raphael: Right. And I also do not believe in this idea of being eloquent with God.

The only way for a human being to realize the full impact

of God is not to be there. Your ego should not be there. Everything should totally dissipate into God to a point where when you look for yourself within his existence, you don't see yourself. It is God who sees you.

Mark: So, let me make sure I have this straight. When you pray, rarely do you get down on your knees and beg for stuff like I do.

Raphael: No. I never do.

Mark: Like, "Please God! Just this one thing."

Raphael: Yes. Never. The minute I do that I am assuming that we are separate, that God does not know where I am or what is bothering me.

Mark: And so when you pray my way you're assuming that God needs your explanations.

Raphael: That he needs an invitation. You see, I do not make appointments with God. My doors are always open. In fact I have no doors. God and I are one whole studio apartment. Whatever I cook, he knows. Wherever I sleep, he knows. I have no privacy at all. And so I do not call God when I am in dire need, because I am always in dire need anyway. It is just useless to describe to God a situation about which he is more aware than I am. It is an indirect admission of his . . .

Mark: Non-omnipotence.

Raphael: Exactly. Look. On a Sunday you put on your best clothes and you go to visit God. And when you come home you take off your good clothes and put on your ragged clothes and along with them comes your ragged behavior. But if you were to make your entire life a celebration, with the same elegant sartorials you wear when you are with God. If you were to wear the same clothes so that there would be no difference between a Sunday and Saturday. And you are always clothed in that; in that behavior, in that self. What a world it would be.

Sue just walked into my office and said that nobody is going to have time to read a Christmas letter that is ten pages long. "They have all year to read it," I respond. "A year isn't as long as it used to be," she counters. She's got me there. By the time you get this far in the letter, the Niners will be toe-tagging the Browns in the Super Bowl. (I know some of you think you're watching Dallas and Pittsburgh, but forget it. Sue's from Cleveland. She begged God to let them in the Super Bowl and God said OK.)

And after the Super Bowl it will be Valentine's Day. Then Easter. We'll probably miss summer again this year because of the suburban riots that will take place when Simpson is acquitted. Then Thanksgiving will be here and before you know it we're right back to Christmas, again. It's not so much that time is shortening, of course, it's just that there are so many more cool events and cataclysms crammed into it these days than when we were young, before, say, three-way traffic signals became the rule. Time isn't shorter. It's just more dense, so it seems shorter. Life, in fact, is sort of getting squeezed out as we try to fit in all the sporting events and the tabloid TV shows. So, I think it's important, especially during the five or six minutes we have to actually enjoy Christmas, to do what Raphael suggests.

First, forgive everybody. Start with your pets. "I'm sorry, Fergie, for screaming at you when you crapped on the new carpet." See how good you feel, now. Next, forgive your brothers and sisters for embezzling your inheritance. I know, it's hard, but do it. And forgive the pond scum lawyers, too. Now, forgive your ex-wife. Hey, you've either got to kill her or forgive her. If you kill her, it's twenty-five years to life. If you forgive her, it's life everlasting, like being at the Coliseum with The Three Tenors, Sinatra and Ronald Reagan, only it never ends. Now, forgive those IRS guys. Come on. They were only doing their job, and you knew when you did it that you can't depreciate your sidewalks. Forgive your neighbors now for keeping their garage door open all the time and ruining your view. Forgive your partners for dropping the ball and screwing up the deal of a lifetime. Forgive your sellers for going psychotic at the last minute and taking away your house in Laguna Beach. Forgive the ones you love for all their neglect and the ones that love you for making you feel like John Gotti. Forgive all the white people for taking over the land, and all the black people for taking over the NBA, and all the Asians for taking over the universities, and all the Hispanics for taking over the AM radio stations, and forgive all your kids for taking over your life. Forgive your coworkers for being so slow and insensitive. Forgive your postal service for throwing your mail in the ravine. Forgive your bank for their vile hidden fees. Forgive the sixties for writing all the good songs and forgive the rappers for only having crap left to write. Forgive the networks and advertisers and Geraldos for making a toilet of the airwaves and forgive your neighbors for paying them to do it. Forgive the Rams, and the Clippers, and the Orange County Board of Supervisors. Now forgive me, even though I didn't do anything. Now, forgive yourself. That's right. Do it now, forgive yourself for everything you've ever done that was rude, and untruthful and low, like those unfair things you said about me behind my back. You are forgiven. I am forgiven. Can you believe it: O.J. is forgiven? The whole world is forgiven.

That is what Christmas is all about. That is what Raphael was talking about. Now, you take that good feeling of forgiveness; you take the moment of grace that you feel right now and let it inform your next moment, and then you let that moment inform the next, and that one the next, and that's what prayer is, right, Raphael? And that's what I wish for everyone this Christmas, a long and prayerful season, one after another, like a Nessun Dorma that never ends.

Until next Christmas (which will be here in about 20 minutes), God bless you.

Mark and Sue and Lara and Fergie

1994
Important Events

- **NAFTA is approved.**

  Lara falls in love.

- **Tonya Harding hires big fat guy to break Nancy Kerrigan's leg.**

  Sue and Mark stop watching figure skating in front of child.

- **Earthquake in L.A. destroys freeway over pass and kills 51 people.**

  Feeling unsafe, Lara creates an escape plan and explains it to parents; sleeps through night for first time.

- **Church of England ordains first women priests.**

  Sue and Mark introduce Lara to Beatles.

- **Amazon.com is launched.**

  Mark invests big in Border's.

- **Sue gets tenure.**

Chores

Mark, Sue, Lara and Fergie
Orange County, California

December 15, 1995

Dear Loved Ones and Others,

Christmas is such a weird season out here in Southern California. At Fashion Island, for example, which is an upscale Newport Beach shopping area the size of Australia, the pristine shoppers walk around in yachting shorts, tennis shorts, shortshorts, or if they're young guys—or want to BE young—in those baggy, ill-proportioned butt-crack shorts you see gang members wear when they're being arrested on TV for shooting their neighbors, or for driving their lowered 1972 Monte Carlos too close to Fashion Island. The bright, warm sun, as if part of the Nieman-Marcus executive gift promotion, shines down on the open-air mall, causing even the koi in the koi ponds to squint their eyes a little as they rise to the surface for handouts of quiche and shitake mushrooms. The whole place shimmers in a warm consumer confidence that adds to the Christmas spirit like zeros to the right of the decimal point. There's even a new niche-market Christmas boutique that sells nothing but sunscreens. The store is bustling with perspiring white patrons buying sunscreen for under the makeup; over the makeup; for skulls and cleavage; for the young, middle-aged, and chronologically challenged. None of this, of course, is that weird for Southern California. We've been this way ever since Annie Hall came out. What's weird is the music.

While I'm sweating in this sunscreen boutique, fighting with wives of yacht brokers and bankrupt Orange County real estate developers for the last tube of "Total Eclipse" that blocks out the entire electromagnetic spectrum, I hear the sound of sleigh bells and the voice of Bing Crosby begins to sing "Frosty the Snowman." "Frosty the Snowman," I think to myself. Isn't that a little weird? But hey, we're cool here. We flow in SoCal. Have to. The song even cheers me up a little. I release my tube of "Total Eclipse" to the nice lady with the sutured cheeks and walk outside. In the blazing sun, I look up at the Christmas tree that's as tall as the World Trade Center and I start to feel pretty good. I think of the people in Cleveland (Sue's hometown) where the temperatures are so cold that all the subatomic particles east of the Ohio River, neutrinos included, have stopped moving. Next thing you know, I'm like everyone else: feeling pretty "normal" in my butt-crack pants, dripping with sweat and gleefully humming the melody to "Let it Snow."

And let's face it: it's been another weird year for us here, hasn't it? We let O.J. go free. We let the L.A. Rams go to St. Louis. And UCI (University of California at Irvine) got caught hawking human eggs to infertile couples. But that's nothing compared to *The Bridges of Madison County*. Did you see that movie? It turned out to be pretty good, which—when you think of the novel—proves that Clint Eastwood is God, and that there are still lots of miracles to be had in the world.

The big surprise for us, though, wasn't that O.J. got away with murder or that our university created a black market for female ovum. The thing that surprised us was the cost of window valences. Man! I couldn't believe it. We bought this new house in July; went from a little three-bedroom abode that I referred to as "quaint" and Sue referred to as "cramped" to a house that's so big we had to put numbers on the all the doors so we could explain to each other where we were going when we walked up stairs. "I'll be in A6, sweetheart, if you need me." "OK, Honey. Lara and I are going to take a shower in C12 and then we'll watch a little TV in the lounge." The ceilings are so high that the house echoes when you walk in the door and even the hamster has a room of its own. E6, I think it is.

I have to admit there are some advantages to moving into the bigger house. Plenty of room inside the closet to put on your shorts and socks, for one thing. That's something we never had in our little place. The echoing ceilings are good, too, for singing "You've Lost that Loving Feeling" in the foyer. I sound as good as both Righteous Brothers. And there's the waterfall. I mean it's not actually a waterfall, but in the two-story house after you take a bath and pull the plug to let out the water, you can run down stairs and listen to it drain down the pipes inside the wall. It sounds just like Niagara Falls. The big disadvantage, of course, is you can't vacuum the whole house from one electrical outlet anymore. The cord used to reach to every room in the house, but now vacuuming is like painting the Golden Gate Bridge; by the time you're finished, it's time to start over again.

The day we moved into the new house was the day we began to make changes to it. In came the French doors; out went the $8 zillion. Down came the wall between the bedrooms, up went the VISA card. Landscape: $2 bazillion not including grass, which they call "turf." Furniture for all the new rooms: $6 gazillion. Paint: $1 gazillion. Crown molding: $85 zillion. Drapes: $12 million a yard, not including valences. Valences: Hey. You don't even want to know about the custom-made valences. Pretty soon every stranger in Orange County had heard about our remodeling effort and started calling us with one indispensable service after another. Finally, we just put a message on our telephone answering machine.

> "If you would like to have some of our money, press one now.
>
> If you already have some of our money, but would like more, please press two now."

And then the contractors heard about our plans, whoa: fifty of them pacing outside our door at night, howling like the coyotes in the hills for a contract to tear our new house apart.

We got estimates from several of them before we started the work. Art Kane was a nice old guy who had retired after building the Union Pacific railroad. He was just picking up pocket change now, doing remodeling work for some of the Chinese landlords in Murietta. We liked him a lot, but it turned out he was more interested in his invention than in changing the two small bedrooms into one big enough for Lara's track and field practice. Art had created a device that would convert the standard American commode into a sort of European bidet. "American women will love it," he said as he showed me the picture of the strange contraption that squirts warm water up your privates while you're going to the bathroom. "Guys, too."

Gordon was great. He tended to see the finished work in his mind's eye better than any of the other contractors we spoke with. A real artist, but a little confused. If I asked one question, he offered six or seven answers that were all so complicated that after a session with him Sue and I had to sit down and watch some "Mayberry RFD" to help us calm down.

Then we met Joe Byrne, the Irishman. He tells me this joke about brain transplants:

"The doctor tells the patient that there's some good news and some bad. "The bad news," he says, "is you have a brain tumor the size of a golf ball. It's terminal." "What's the good news?" asks the patient. "The good news is we can now do brain transplants. All you have to do is decide which kind of brain you would like." "Great," says the patient who was much relieved. "What are my choices?" "Well, you can have this American brain, but I don't recommend it." The patient asks why and the doctor says American brains are all worn out from overwork and stress. "Or you can have this British brain, but I don't recommend it either." "Why not?" asks the patient. "The British brains are a little worn too, from thinking too much and using all those big words." Finally, the doctor pulls out an Irish brain and shows it to the patient. "This is an Irish brain," he says. "This is the one I would recommend." The patient asks the doctor why he would recommend the Irish brain. "Because," says the doctor, "It's never been used."

When I asked him how he would proceed with the remodel, he says, "We'll just tear it down and then doctor it up a bit." That sounded pretty good, so we hired Joe.

On the day before the guys arrived to install the French doors, Joe came over and prepared the holes in the wall. Lara was there watching him. I told her that Joe was from the country where the leprechauns come from and that maybe he had seen one. "Ask him," I said. "No. You ask him," she replies in a whisper. "I'm not going to ask him," I say, again. "You have to ask him." "No way. You ask him." "No, you." "No you." "You." "Now I'm getting curious myself," Joe interjects. "What is it you want to ask?" Lara is very shy. She hesitates and then slowly poses the question. "Have you ever seen a leprechaun?"

"Oh yes," says Joe. "I've seen a bunch of them and the fairies, too."

He tells us about the village in Ireland where he was born. Translated from the Gaelic, the name of the village means "land of the fairies" and they're not kidding about this stuff. The little people are as real to the Irish as, say, equity is to an American. He told us about the time he caught a leprechaun. "You know the little people are very tricky," he explains. "If you take your eyes off of them while you have them caught, they disappear, just like that." And he snaps his fingers. He says he had one in the palm of his hand and was ready to force him to give up the three wishes that leprechauns have to give you if you catch them. "I had him right here in my hand," he says. Lara's eyes are as big as bicycle wheels. "I was thinking of the wishes I was going to get out of him. There was one of those ancient castles behind me; the kind you see all over Ireland, and just when I was going to get my wish the little guy said, 'Look! The castle is on fire.' I turned my head and looked and when I turned back, he was gone." Lara was entranced. "The interesting thing was the castle actually was on fire at the time," Joe concluded. He has that Irish genius for keeping the fires of enchantment alive in a child (and of course within himself, as well). We were lucky that he combined this genius with a talent for tearing things down and doctoring them back up again.

"How long is it?" Sue asks. "No. Not that. The Christmas letter." She wants to know how long the Christmas letter is. "Oh," I say. "I think it's about four pages single spaced. "That's good enough," she replies. "They don't want to read any more than four pages about our room addition." "But I haven't told them about Lara's reading group yet, and the Cleveland Indians, and my new computer. I have to tell them about my Pentium chip."

Sue is the kind of person that goes right to the point with things as long as it is not unpleasant, in which case she ignores it completely. Me, I like to take the long way around the barn. "Honey," I say. "These people wait all year to find out what reading group Lara is in. We can't disappoint them."

Lara, of course, turned six in November. A couple of days before her birthday Sue walked into our bedroom sobbing. Sue never sobs. The last time I saw her really weeping was when *Cheers* went off the air. But she was sobbing now and it scared me. What did I do, now?

"What is it, Honey?" I say, hoping that I hadn't forgotten our anniversary again, or left my dirty socks on the bed. "Lara only has a few more weeks to be five," she says, tears running down her face. "She has been so cute at five years old. It has gone so fast. And pretty soon she won't be five years old anymore." Whew! What a relief! This must be one of those gender-specific emotions I've heard so much about. I hold her in my arms for a moment and say something profoundly consoling, like, "Six will be good, too, honey. We'll make her stay cute. If she doesn't stay cute, we'll turn her in for something with fur."

We introduced Lara to the concept of chores this year. In fact, we called for a family meeting to do it. "Lara!" I yell upstairs to C9. "Come down here. We need to talk about your chores!" She comes down. "I was playing school," she says in an accusatory way, as if I had interrupted her study for the LSAT. Then she asks, "What's a chore?"

We explain the concept. We talk about homework and the need to establish some kind of routine. Lara actually gets enthused about the idea. As we brainstorm the chores for which she will be responsible, things like paying the bills, doing the shopping and changing the transmission in the BMW, she begins to perceive some real potential for new "play."

"Homework," says Sue. And she writes it down on the white board with a bright red marker. Lara says "Make my bed!" Yes, cleaning up your room is a good one I say. "Taking the dishes off the table," pipes in Sue and writes it down. Pretty soon we have five or six chores written in bright primary colors on the white board. "Ok, now write the days of the week across the top." I draw horizontal lines to create rows for the chores and vertical lines to create columns for the days of the week. Lara says she wants to draw the lines, so I hand her the marker. Hey! This is fun! Once the grid is created, we explain that every day, each cell of the grid should have a check or "x" inside of it to indicate that the chore has been done that day. By the end of the week, the entire grid should be filled.

"Shall we use checks or X's?" I ask. Lara draws a check on the board. I show her how the tail should be a little longer. Making checks on the board is a blast. After the chart has been completed, Sue says, "What happens if she doesn't finish her chores?" We look at each other. Huh?

It's not as easy as it sounds. We can't take away TV because we don't watch it enough and we certainly don't want to make it a reward. What else? We draw a blank. It's not like we can take away her car or cancel the trust fund. She loves school, but it would be pretty lame to say if you don't finish your homework you can't go to school. We are genuinely stymied. We can't think of anything to deny her if her chores aren't done. Then it comes to me. "I know," I say. "She loves these chores, so if she doesn't finish them, we'll take THEM away."

Sue gives me that wifelook, the one Eve gave Adam when he brought home the snake and told her it was a pet. Long Pause. OK. OK. So let's rethink the whole thing.

Cleveland got into the World Series for the first time in decades. That may not be a big deal for you, but it was for Sue. The last year the Indians won the pennant was the year that Sue was born, and legend has it that while her mom was in labor at the hospital, her dad was at the game.

I remember the first game in the Series that they won. It had gone on for what seemed like a couple of weeks. It was tied up, six to six in the ninth. Sue was riveted to the tube like I have never seen her before. I put Lara to bed. I took a shower. I read a couple of novels, solved the Rubik Cube and when I got back downstairs the game was still going on. Finally, Atlanta walked Bell, knowing that Eddie Murray, who had gone oh-for-five in the game, would be batting next. Big mistake. There was a guy on second. Murray cracked a base hit over second base and that was it. The game was over. Sue had been sick for a couple of days, but Cleveland had laid on the hands. She was healed. "We're still in it," she screamed as she jumped up and down. "We're still in it! We're still in it! We're still in it!" I hadn't seen her so excited since I put that potato down my pants. And that's kind of how I feel about life, too. (Not the potato. That was a joke.) "Being in it." I mean. I think if you stay in the game, good things can happen.

"Buffalos!" One of the construction guys had taken a pair of binoculars out to the back yard and scanned the horizon. "Buffalos," he said, with a surprised tone. "I thought they were buffaloes and they ARE buffaloes."

Sometimes Christmas really gets me down because we get so

stressed out and overburdened by our obligations that we seem to lose the enchantment. But every year I feel this way and every year something happens to break through the shell of skepticism. This year it was the buffaloes. Our new house is close to a mountain. There are lots of houses around, but the Cleveland National Forest is behind us and that's nice because the land will probably remain free of developers for a while. Red-tailed hawks sail over head. Roadrunners prance across the backyard. Coyotes come down from the hills at night and feed on the housecats. But buffaloes? I don't believe it. "Give me those binoculars," I say to Alwyn (he's from England. That's why his name is that way.) I scan the horizon. Down in the canyon, behind a thick grove of oaks, I see this big black head. Then another one. Buffaloes. Three, four, maybe five buffaloes. We've got buffaloes on our land! How enchanting can it get?

Then Lara comes into the office with the Christmas list I asked her to write. She hands it to me. I'm thinking maybe dolls, a pair of sunglasses, a few days at the Ritz Carlton. Here's what Lara is asking for Christmas: Real magic fairy dust, real wings, real magic wands, real flying dust, and real disappearing dust (so I can make Robbie disappear).

With the Buffaloes and Fairy Dust and Lara's indubitable belief in magic, the enchantment of Christmas flows back into my life. I love it, again. The faith, the fantasy, the saving grace of it all. But where in the heck am I going to get "real" flying dust?

I better stop writing and start looking. (Believe me, she's not kidding about the dust.) And sure, it's been a weird year with O.J., and the Rams, and the black market embryos, but that's just tabloid stuff. Don't ever believe that what you see in the media is reality. It's not even close. Reality is not what's on television, it's what you allow in your heart and in your house. We hope yours is full of rainbows, leprechauns, fairy dust and maybe a few buffaloes.

Till next year, Merry Christmas!

Mark, Sue, Lara & Fergie

1995
Important Events

- **Concept of World Wide Web enters popular vocabulary.**

  Sue and Mark still trying to figure out "Martha Stewart" concept. Lara explains html to parents.

- **At 2,131, Cal Ripken, Jr breaks Lou Gehrig's record for consecutive games played.**

  Mark crosses goal off list.

- **Still, nine out of ten Americans have not yet logged onto the Internet.**

  Sue asks Lara what "logged on" means.

- **O.J. is acquitted.**

  Lara completes her first chore.

- **Dow closes above 5,000 for first time, ever.**

  Mark calls for patience. "It will come down and then we'll buy.

The Year of Shoes and Swallows

Mark, Sue, Lara and Fergie
Orange County, California

December 20, 1996

Dear Friends, Family, and Inmates,

Probably the most noteworthy thing about living in Southern California this year is that nothing noteworthy has happened. Generally speaking, we have a reputation for being in the spotlight and setting national trends. We started the telephone psychic networks trend, for example, the beach volleyball trend, the *Baywatch* rerun trend, and more recently the trend to install those electronically controlled toll roads that debit you're checking account every time you change lanes (We built two of them in Orange County this year.). These are cultural contributions that can be traced directly to the enlightened citizens, right here in Southern California.

When we're not setting trends, we try to make headlines with our "disaster thing." Remember back in '93 when we had the riots and fires. First, South Central Los Angeles burned, then Malibu and Laguna Beach went up in flames. Then, when our house was threatened, we called the fire department and they put it out. It was an exciting time for all of us and especially noteworthy because it was the first time ever that guys like Rodney King and Peter Uberroth could be found in the same line applying for your tax dollars to rebuild their homes. In '94 we had the O.J. trial—which was declared a national disaster the day after Marsha Clarke changed her hairdo.

This year, however, I can't think of anything that's happened here that's worth the banner on a supermarket tabloid. No earthquakes. No riots. No infernos. Not even much in the way of murders—true, we had the Linda Sobek trial, but it came and went so fast I don't think there was even a T-shirt for that one. No. It's been very quiet around here, but in an uncanny way, we're still setting the trend for the rest of the world, because nothing much has happened out there either. If you think about it, nothing has really happened since the fall of the Berlin Wall. What, for example, are the big issues facing the nation today? Do we balance the budget by the time Lara is ten years old, or do we stretch it out until she's twelve? Whoa! That one has me pacing the floor at night. Shall we put phonics back in the classroom, or just ask the Asians to read stuff to us. Or what about national security? Do we bring home the troops from Bosnia, or just send them down to Rwanda to help the Hutus and Tutsis. Oh well, let's go to Mars, then, where there might be some life.

Come on, you guys. Where are the mega-events we used to have? Like the Cuban Missile Crisis, the oil embargoes, wild revolutionary uprisings in third-world countries, and Starsky and Hutch on Wednesday nights. Is this what world peace is all about: the Switzerlandization of the entire human race? Before you know it, we'll be arguing about how many holes to put in the cheese. I make these comments only as a way of saying that our news this year—which, as far as we are concerned, is the important news anyway—has been as tepid and uneventful as the world at large.

Sue and I worked up an order for some new Tupperware, and WOW! What a change that has made in our lives. Then we got the piano tuned. And that was enough excitement for the first quarter. I finally gave in to high fashion this year, too and invested in some cool pants "for the bigger-butted man." I look a lot better now and it's much easier than going to the gym. With the new designer EXPANDO pants, I can exhale again, which I haven't done since about the third grade. True, these are not the big events one would normally put into a Christmas letter, but for us it's been a year of small accomplishments, like getting up, getting Lara up, and getting the safety cap off our jars of energy-enhancing supplements that are stuffed with exotic herbs with names like ginkgo biloba.

Sue and I have both been very busy at work, too. Sue has been recruiting laid-off aerospace engineers (rocket scientists) to teach reading and math to felons at the Orange County Jail. It's not an easy job convincing guys who went to M.I.T. for six years that it will be a lot better for them and their families if they drop all that rocket science stuff and instead teach our local criminals how to add. But if anybody can do it, Sue can. She just looks at them with her big blue eyes and explains that it was no coincidence that the downsizing of the aerospace industry coincided almost perfectly with the dramatic expansion of our prisons. "The real challenges aren't in outer space anymore," she says with a soft, irresistible sincerity. "They're in prison." And somehow, for some reason, they believe her and sign up.

I'm finishing my novel, producing CDs, videos and a lot of other corporate communications that are creating record sales for my clients. I also submitted my ideas on string theory to the National Academy of Sciences. But to tell you the truth, most of our time has been spent looking for Lara's shoes. No. It's true.

For our family, it's been the year of the shoe.

As children like Lara grow up and mature, parents like us make some gains and suffer some losses. Kids become much more mobile and self-sufficient, like they can breathe on their own and do potty and stuff by the time they are six or seven. Studies have shown, however, that kids don't really master the idea of shoes until they're about eighteen or nineteen, when they need them to run away from the police. They can get dressed more or less by themselves, and it's not like they don't know how to put on and tie their shoes; it's just that it doesn't occur to them until it's too late.

Here's how it works. Since the kids are older now, they have to go to a lot more places like school, piano, singing, Girl Scouts, and political action committee meetings where they talk about the phonics issue. And that usually means they have to get dressed. We parents have the time factors for each of these venues figured out to the nanosecond. We know what time we have to be where and then we back up and calculate how much time we have to get the child out of what I call "kid-mind" and into what I call "parent-mind," which includes in its notion of reality things like breakfast, vitamins, dressing, brushing teeth and hair, potty, back-pack, sunscreen, etc., etc., etc. We know exactly how much time we can allot to each activity. We add an additional thirty minutes to get from the kitchen to the car (I don't know why, but that's what seems to take the longest), and if we execute all that correctly, we usually arrive at gymnastics on time.

Except, of course, for the shoes. Just when you think you have successfully executed your plan for getting into the car—a plan no less complicated than the one used by the U.S. Defense Department to invade Iraq—you look down at your child's feet (in my case, Lara's feet), and you say, with a slight hint of panic,

"Where are your shoes?"

Lara, who has not yet moved completely out of "kid-mind" with its unlimited time dimension and into "parent-mind" with its relentless scheduling demands, responds by saying, "Huh?" "Where are your shoes, honey?" I say again. "I don't know," she says. "Well, where did you leave them, darling?" Lara furrows her brow and says, "I think I left them . . ." Then she drifts back into kid-mind and starts to stand on her head.

For a parent, this can be a terrifying experience. The clock is ticking, and we have no idea where the shoes are. We begin our search. Calmly, at first. I run upstairs to her room, look in the closet, under the bed, and behind the chest. In the meantime, Lara starts shaking the pennies out of her gumball machine. I look in the office, under the desk, in the waste basket and behind the bookcase. No shoe. Then the bathroom, yes! The left shoe is there: right in the bathtub where she left it. "Lara, I found one shoe, do you know where the other one is?"

The multi-colored gumballs are rolling all over the kitchen floor. "Huh?" she says. Jesus, it's getting late. "Where's your god-damn shoe, Lara, honey?" I respond. "I'm cleaning up," she says. Of course, she is not cleaning up, but she knows that it will be harder for me to tell her to stop cleaning up than it would be for me to tell her to stop playing around with her gum machine. So, she says she's cleaning up, which is a totally unethical tactic.

"Lara, honey, if you don't put that gum away and help me find your other shoe then we're not going to piano and you'll spend the rest of the day in your room. "I'm coming. I'm coming. Geez, Dad! I was just cleaning up," she says like I'm being irrational. I look in the kitchen pantry for the other shoe. In the cupboard where we keep the dishes. Under the sink where we keep the monolithic box of Cascade from Price Club. I know you probably think these are unlikely places for a kid's shoe, but if you think that then you don't have any kids, or if you do, then they don't have feet. In the closet with the vacuum cleaner. Under the couch. In the dog's box. Inside the piano. No damn shoe. Lara has slipped back into kid-mind and is doing some origami with the paper napkins that I threw on the floor while rummaging through the pantry.

"Lara, if you don't help me find that shoe, then I'm going to tear both your arms off and beat you over the head with them." "Geez, Dad, I'm looking. I thought it might be under these napkins."

I go outside and look in the flowerbeds. I look over the fence in the neighbor's yard. I climb the tree and look in the branches. But no shoe and the parent-mind factor is bearing down even more, now.

As any parent knows, if, after spending two to three hours getting your child ready to go somewhere you fail to get the child into the car within a five-minute period after completing the last task necessary for departure, then the law of reverse readiness kicks in. What that means is the kid's state of readiness begins quickly to degrade. First, the jacket comes off. Then the hair things fall out of the hair and it starts looking like it did when the kid woke up. Then she spills something on her T-shirt. Within minutes you're back to where you began several hours ago. And this is what was beginning to happen to Lara. So, I have to take some extreme action.

She's balancing herself like a tightrope walker on the little brick wall that lines the patio. "Lara, dammit! If you don't get your jacket back on and get in the car this minute, I'm going to take you to school in my underwear. I know that will get her going. "Geez, Dad. I was just practicing my gymnastics." "Practice walking to the car." "But I only have one shoe." "You don't need shoes to play the piano. Just get in the car."

I pick her up in my arms and carry her to the garage. I open the door of the car and toss her in. Then I toss in her left shoe. Then I climb in and slam the door. We have thirty seconds to get to piano lessons. I click the garage door opener and while trying to think of what to say to the piano teacher about Lara's bare feet, I look down at the floor on the shotgun side of the car and what do you think I see: that's right, Lara's other shoe.

"There's your shoe," I scream somewhat hysterically. "I know," she responds, cool and calm. She had taken it off during our last trip in the car and then hopped inside the house on one foot. "Geertz!" I say. It was a close call, but we made it, and Lara's playing the piano pretty well now, with or without her shoes.

OK. You're saying to yourself about now, "Geeez, this Christmas letter is getting long." Or, "Do I really care that much about Lara's shoes?" Don't think I haven't heard these complaints before. I hear them all the time. But I want to tell you, complaints only make it harder on the other readers, because the more complaints I get, the longer I make the letter. That's right. This is more than just a Christmas letter. It's also a team-building exercise, like being in the Marines. We all just have to pitch in and read our part and get through it together as best we can—Semper Fi—and if one person breaks down and complains (or, worse yet: doesn't finish), well, everybody is going to suffer. In the long run you'll all feel better about yourselves, and have the added satisfaction of discovering what my favorite movie was for 1996.

After everything I've said about Lara's shoes, it may not be obvious to you how gifted she is. But she is, and we have the papers to prove it. She was admitted to what they call the "GATE" program at her school, which is an advanced class that is supposed to be more challenging. For a while these "gifted" kids didn't seem all that smart. It wasn't until Thanksgiving that we really got a taste of how off-the-charts they were.

The class was performing a little play about the Puritans and the Indians. At one point each child stood up and told the audience the things for which they were thankful. It started off with some pretty routine things; I'm thankful for my mom and dad because they love me so much; for my dog because he makes me happy; for my toys, because they're better than the kid's next door. When little Warren stood up, dressed in his Hiawatha outfit, however, things changed.

"I'm thankful for the electromagnetic spectrum, because without the low-end frequencies we wouldn't have the color blue." Then Seth stands up and says he's thankful for fusion because if we didn't have fusion there wouldn't be a sun and without the sun we would all die. These were little second-graders dressed up like Cotton Mather telling an audience of worn out middle-class parents with bowling scars how thankful they were for neutrinos, differential equations and the general theory of relativity, "because it means when we approach the speed of light, time will slow down and we can play Nintendo for infinity." Lara is gifted, but not like that. I think she's more gifted in the area of convincing the school psychologist into thinking she knows the answers to questions for which she really hasn't a clue. Good gift, though.

Here's a sample of how her mind is working these days. I was explaining to her about the democratic process, how all the people in the country decide together who is going to be the leader. I tried to explain the word "election". I told her how Bob Dole and Bill Clinton were trying to convince all the people in the country that they are the best one to be in charge. I said democracy was basically like everybody in the country just raising their hands for one guy or the other. "When you grow up you can run for president, too; if you want to," I said encouragingly. Lara thought for a minute. Then said, "I'd have to get a husband." Oh, my god! What a blow that was. I mean we so wanted Lara to be at least a little bit liberated. "Why do you need a husband?" I said, with not-so-subtle regret.

And she says, "Someone has to stay home with the baby."

As you can tell, Sue and I have been splitting up the parenting process fifty-fifty, which is what a lot of feminists have been proposing for a long time. It sounds like a good idea. The male gets the satisfaction of being an active participant in the "realtime" development of the child, while also holding down a sixty-hour a week career. But once a man bonds with his child, his professional life goes south, which of course is part of the feminist five-year plan. What he gives up in professional achievement, prestige, bonuses, and net worth is supposed to be made up by the rich relationship he establishes with the pharmacist, kindergarten teacher, PTA members, Spanish-speaking au pairs that he meets at the swing set, and maybe even the child. It's true, the male in this process discovers things about himself that he would never have known had he devoted himself one hundred percent to his work like his successful friends have done. For example, he never would have thought himself capable of substituting the word potty for his rich repertoire of particularly edgy "male" bodily-function phrases. But there you go: potty, potty, potty, potty!

And, as satisfying as it is, and it is, there are some definite downsides. Here's an example of how it can affect your relationship with colleagues.

I arrive at corporate headquarters for a meeting with four or five no-nonsense males who have double-nonfat cappuccinos with extra ginkgo and a .05mg of testosterone before coming to work. These guys are tough. They're in sales. They spend the morning admiring the girth of their hair follicles and imagining that they could still be one of those Calvin Klein male briefs models if they wanted to, if they hadn't decided instead to sell chalk for a living.

I, of course, spent my morning looking for Lara's shoes and deciding whether she should wear the socks with the little bears on them or the blue . We meet at the conference room where we all make an effort to establish ourselves as aggressive, can-do kinds of guys. As a greeting, Nate tries to slug me in the shoulder, but misses and hits me in the side of the head. I show no pain. He asks whether I've heard the score, and I immediately say yeah, six to nine. Hey that's a good one, he says, six to nine. Sixty-nine, get it?

John reaches down to the crotch of his Zapata slacks and gives his gonads a little lift. "Helen and I went out last night," he says. "Had a gooooooooooooooood time." We all nod and grin. Nate slugs John. Barry steps up and shakes everyone's hand. "Morning," he says, and as he squeezes your hand you can see the pinstripes over his pectorals swell like a special effect. The pain in your hand is the kind that makes spies talk. I show no sign of pain, though; just nod; then give my own gonads a lift. (Hey, they were there a minute ago.).

The Vice President of Sales approaches—he's the decision maker in this group, the boss—and we all move from locker room mode to kiss-ass mode. Mr. Jameson greets us. Nice suit, Don. Don says thanks. Says his wife picked it up in Milan when she was there last month adopting children from the Russian breakaway republics. She's a wonderful woman, Don. Don says thanks. Then the boss says shall we get this thing underway?

And here's where my parenting life has a head-on collision with the professional rapport I have worked so hard to attain with my colleagues. John opens the door to the conference room and as the guys begin to enter, I all of a sudden find myself opening my mouth and saying, "Wait a minute. Before we go in, don't you think you should go potty?

It just slipped out, but it would have done less harm to my reputation as a serious sports-minded guy if I had farted like a horse. All the guys froze in their tasseled loafers and stared at me. Then they looked at Mr. Jameson. Mr. Jameson turned his head slowly in my direction with what I interpreted as a kind of executive death-ray countenance and said, "I went potty at home." It was out of my hands now. Since he was responding precisely as Lara does I can't help but respond in kind, and in doing so destroy any chance of picking up this contract or ever exchanging cigars or blows with any of these sales guys again. I said, "You wipe good?"

But it is worth it. It's worth it to see your daughter lying on the front lawn on a weekday morning staring up at the swallows and naming each one as it swoops down from the sky. That's something that happens around here every year. The swallows return. And it's one of those events that makes a somewhat uneventful year quite eventful after all. One day they're not here. And the next day, there are hundreds of them dive-bombing the house and making nests in the eaves. Their wings are shaped like little boomerangs and they swoop through the air at such peculiar acrobatic angles that it's hard to follow them. "There's one," I say to Lara and point. "There's one!" she says back. I still don't know what a swallow looks like in the perched position, because they're always darting through the sky like airborne pinballs. Their birdsong is unusual, too: sounding more like a dolphin than a bird. And for some reason they are a truly welcome sight. Nice to have them back.

On that day, Lara wanted to watch television, but of course I said no, and once it sank in that she wasn't going to sit and stare at the TV, her natural imaginative powers kicked in and she went outside and discovered the swallows. She sat on the grass and started giving them names according to their style of flight. "There's Swoopy," she says. "There's Up-and-Down." I sat next to her for a while and looked up, too. "There's Roundy! Zippy and Flash!"

The garden was another event for us. We wanted Lara to know that food came from the ground instead of Pavilions, so we got some dirt and some seeds and started planting. In fact, we may have over-planted a little. Since this was our first time farming, we planted everything we could find that had a seed: peas, radishes, carrots, broccoli, spinach, onions, scallions, beets, lettuce, tons of tomatoes, pumpkins (the vine of which would eventually eat the cat next door), squash, sweet peppers and sunflowers. Unfortunately, we planted them all the same day, so they ripened all at once, too: on August 3. We ate salad every day 'til October, and still had enough zucchini to make methane fuel for the car.

Lara saw a ghost, too. No. It's true. We were just driving along and out of nowhere she says, "I saw a ghost, Dad." I asked her where she saw the ghost. She says in the backyard. "His back was toward me. He was facing the gate. I just stood there and looked at it for a while and then it just disappeared." And I think I believe her. What do you think? Do you think kids see things that adults cannot see? Do you think dads are prejudiced about their daughters? Maybe a little. But it is really cool and still a little mysterious to watch and be part of Lara's unfolding. She's growing more complex, gaining definition, insights, tons of humor, and a glow. All of a sudden, the word comes to me: Style! Lara's getting a style. Even in the hospital.

It was last June. A Friday. Lara had been coughing non-stop for about sixteen hours and her cold—as it sometimes does—began to develop into asthma. We'd been through this many times before. We're pretty good at controlling it with drugs and steroids, but this time we were overwhelmed. We'd been giving her the nebulizer every two hours with very little relief. She coughs and coughs and coughs and the wheezing becomes monstrous.

By now, it is Saturday morning about 2 a.m. Lara is pleading with us. "Please! I need the machine, now. Please give me the machine." "We can't give you the machine sweetheart. Not for another hour." If we give her any more of this medicine it could stop her heart. Yet without it, she coughs this dry, fruitless cough and struggles for breath. Sue and I ache with fear and helplessness.

We turn off the lights. I look for some candles. Come on! Where are the damn candles, I think to myself, but I don't say anything. The whole point of the candles is to try to create a relaxed atmosphere, to relax the spasms. Sue holds Lara in her arms, rocks her for hours. I light one candle. I get the second candle lit, but the wick of the third candle is broken and the flame crawls up the stem of the match toward my finger and burns me before I can get the candle started. And here's what I mean about style. Lara can't breathe. I'm going nuts trying to get the candle lit and what does she say? "Don't worry, Dad. I can do with two candles."

In the candlelight we play soft, choral music, me in the chair in a catatonic state, Sue rubbing Lara's back on the couch as she pleads for the machine, trying to calm her, trying to save her life. We're on the phone back and forth with our doctor, calling him at home, paging him: Shall we give her the steroids? Can we give her more Albuterol? Finally we give up and take her to the emergency room.

We got things under control—or at least we thought we did—and brought her back home, but by five-thirty in the morning she was coughing and wheezing again, uncontrollably. This had never happened before. We just couldn't get it under control; couldn't get our helpless arms around this monster.

After she coughed for twenty-four hours straight, we took her back to the emergency room at nine a.m., and, over my heartbroken objections, she was admitted at about eleven o'clock. She was there for about four or five days. We were just crushed that she would have to go through this, have all these people pumping powerful drugs inside of her over and over again. The drugs caused her to become frenetic, and we had to watch her turn into this amped little zombie who couldn't do much more than stare straight ahead. There were tubes stuck in her nose and arms. All she can do was utter little bits and pieces of what she caught floating through her taut little mind, which was throbbing with steroids and high impact drugs that pounded away at her central nervous system. But at least she could breathe. I wanted to take her home, but the doctors kept saying one more day. I think we should keep her here one more day. I think one more day. One more day. Just one more day. I gave up. We failed.

Gradually, Lara did improve and we started riding up and down the hospital corridors with her in a wheel chair and I pushing from behind. We started having fun again, and she said if she could ride the wheelchair like we'd been doing, she wouldn't mind going back.

Although, as I have said, it has been a somewhat uneventful year for us, we still get a lot of vicarious excitement from the interesting lives being led by our friends. Brian, for example, goes to Baywatch location shoots and hangs out with Mayor Giuliani in New York. He proposed to his fiancée over a radio talk show and we're hoping the wedding will be on HBO. Eduardo and Peggy launched their own ad agency; then they had a baby; now they're having another one. Next year they'll have to buy condos for all the au pairs. Michael, my Beverly Hills hair guy, went to India to find enlightenment and came back with pictures of this gorgeous woman with whom he had apparently attained some form of satori. Merry is studying Spanish down in Boca Raton so she can relate more effectively with her Cuban colleagues. She helped build the Holocaust Museum in Washington, D.C., and had Hillary Clinton over to her house for lunch; says Hilary has paid a price for her political success. Sunji moved from Carmel to the Rocky Mountains of Colorado where she and Tom built the house they always wanted to build (thank God they finally got out of that rat race in Carmel). Diane and Jimmy went to London to check out the theater at the West End. Their daughter Chelsea got her first part in a musical (she's six). George—with no job or identifiable income—continues to fight over in England for alternative energy sources that do not consume our limited natural resources or pollute the air, earth and water upon which we are all so utterly dependent. Fernando in a very subtle and unobtrusive way is managing his investments and, without their knowing it, raising the consciousness of all the people with whom he comes in contact, except maybe his mother. Ray and his wife are back to the weight they boasted in high school! (I am, too, but I was very fat in high school.) My mother has become a painter. My sister Marsha is helping a ton of people see more clearly the obscure forces that are driving their lives. Jeff and Jill are healing people every day. My brother Mike and my sister-in-law Bonnie are devoting themselves to a nonprofit organization the mission of which is nothing less than a revolution in the way in which adults understand children and the childhood experience. Mike and Bonnie figure if parents see their kids a little differently, then they'll treat them differently, and if they treat them differently, then the kids will grow up differently and then, of course, we'll have a different world in which to live. My dad has been getting written up in the newspaper lately for winning horseshoe tournaments. My other dad up in Seattle has infected the world with a virus called optimism. Once one gets it, there is no cure. Sue's mom (Nana)—you'll all be glad to hear—has reversed the aging process. She's now younger than us all! Robyn has become an artist, without even knowing it. I was watching C-SPAN the other night and saw my old friend Anita. She is now the president of an extremely prestigious woman's political caucus—in fact that might be the name of the organization: the Women's Political Caucus in Washington, D.C. She has taken her compassion—genuine, full-hearted compassion—all the way to the top. Ken finished his screenplay. Now all he needs is $50M to make the movie. But don't think it can't happen. Anything can happen. Raphael is proof of that. You all remember Raphael. He graduated from Harvard Divinity School in August.

So, OK, I was wrong. A lot has been going on this year after all. I just hadn't noticed. It has been, in its way, a very eventful year, at least for everyone but me. And maybe that is going to be the real challenge for us in this unusual post-cold-war period: to keep from Balkanizing and fighting over the number of holes in the cheese; to join together like we did in that utterly inane movie *Independence Day*, but without the evil invaders, without the need to create a big, bad, evil force against which to unite. Can we do that? It's probably impossible—I know it's impossible for guys—but Christmas is a good time to think about this stuff, anyway, with its central notions of forgiveness and love. Yeah, that's probably as good a place to start as any: by forgiving and then loving. I know it's hard, especially for guys, but let's give it a try. See what it feels like to just say OK, I forgive everybody. Just say it to yourself, "I forgive everybody, even Republicans." Just give it up. Whatever they did, they didn't really know what they were doing. I mean wasn't that the message? That as smart as we are, there is still a big block of information about which we know nothing, and that without that knowledge, the things that we do know are utterly incomplete. And so aren't we at best, just guessing? Which opens the door, doesn't it, for forgiveness? And once you forgive all those people around you and then once you forgive yourself, the love will probably come of its own accord. So maybe we just need to forgive. Maybe that will do it. You want to give it a try?

Well, how do you know it won't work? Have you ever tried it? Geeez! What a rectum! No. No. I didn't mean that. I'm sorry. I didn't mean that. I forgive you. I do. I swear to God. I forgive you. I love you. Jesus, this isn't easy, is it?

But you can do it!

Merry Christmas,
With lots of love and forgiveness

Mark, Sue, Lara and Fergie

1996
Important Events

- **Nothing happens in 1996.**

  Lara sees a ghost.

- **President Clinton is reelected.**

  Lara adds the word "duh" to her vocabulary.

- **Concept of "dot" -- as in "dot.com" -- enters popular vocabulary.**

  For first time, Lara finds both shoes in under 30 minutes.

- **President Clinton promises to balance federal budget within seven years.**

  Sue's says ours will take at least that long.

- **NASA launches the Mars Global Surveyor.**

  Sue hires laid off aerospace workers to teach arithmetic to O.C. Jail inmates.

- **Dow breaks 6,000.**

  Mark wary of "irrational exuberance."

The Year of Homework

Mark, Sue, Lara and Fergie
Orange County, California

Christmas 1997

Dear Friends, Celebrities and Loved Ones,

Whew! The holidays are over, thank goodness, and it's a relief to go back to work where one can get some rest. Sorry I'm late with this, but Christmas nailed me. Then we had to return all those gifts (Geeez, what job that can be.). And now there are all those resolutions to write, which I think I've refined down to three key goals: find the zone, enter the zone, and get on TV.

Our community here in southern California could sure do with some "zone" as well. I mean here it is 1998 already and we did nothing last year so far as I can tell to boost the now-flaccid reputation of L.A. and Orange County as the trendsetting center of hype. OK. Brad Pitt and Gwyneth Paltrow split up. That was hot. They're from here and it caused a nice blip on the stylin' detectors. But come on! This is Los Angeles; yet the planet Mars is getting more airtime than we are. Movies are being made about the former Yugoslavia and Tibet; animated features about Rasputin. But what about us? We have guys out here twice as repulsive as Rasputin (see: Orange County Board of Supervisors). But the media is just not picking them up. Do the architects of trend really think we're going to capture the imagination of the global village by putting Danny DeVito in all our movies? I hate to say it, but dude: Where is the Juice when you really need him? We tried to get some race and gender action going last year by passing Proposition 201. Basically, it stated that discriminating according to race or gender was forbidden. But some serious Karma came back to haunt us on that one. An ex-hippy, SDS, nouveau-black-panther judge that Jerry Brown named to the bench back in the seventies got a hold of the proposition and did a double-zen-entendre with its interpretation. He ruled that any law that forbids discrimination according to race or gender is discriminatory, especially to people of race and gender. All my friends from the Balkans stopped calling me after that one came down. "It's like Byzantine, man," they said. "We've had that Byzantine shit for a thousand years. We don't need Byzantine from L.A."

It's a wakeup call, people! L.A. T-shirt sales are off. Our bands are migrating to Prague. If Southern California is going to stay competitive and garner its share of world media, we're going to have to do something totally grotesque.

Which we did. Remember those two paramilitary guys who dressed up like a swat team on a bad hair day. They walk into a bank with automatic assault rifles, grenade launchers, tubes of anthrax and tiny thermonuclear devices that fit in the little zipper pockets of their cool para-military pants. They rob the bank, but they're so loaded down with ordnance that they can't get it all back in the car during their getaway. So they shoot it out with police on TV for about an hour. It was very dramatic. And yes, we got L.A. on CNN. Days of replays. Friends from all around the world were calling for details. How close was the shoot out to the Rockingham Estate? Was Brad Pitt involved? What's the closest restaurant to the crime scene? It was cool. These two guys got us on TV. News ratings took off. Sponsors sold a ton of cat chow. The world saw L.A. again as a city on the edge. And then it all disappeared. And you want to know why? No trial. The two guys died in the shootout.

When the shootout failed, and prop 201 fizzled on us, and then housing starts peaked (bringing nothing but peace and prosperity) the city had to do something to bring back the cameras. So they invented this thing called El Niño. It worked pretty well for a while. Friends were calling in from all over the globe to find out what was going on with El Niño and I told them: sandbag, man. This thing is big; it's affecting alpha waves, net worth, house pets, everything. So sandbag the shit out of your house wherever you live. But no storm came, and so no cameras came either.

Next, we built the Getty Center. Sixteen thousand tons of elegant white cleft-cut Italian travertine stone structures on top of the last undeveloped hill in L.A. Everyone thought it was going to be a very hot art museum until they found out the art consisted mostly of old bedroom furniture from France and some paperback books from the twelfth century.

Desperate circumstances calling for desperate actions, the next move to bring some "story" back to Southern California brought tears to the guys from the Greater L.A. Chamber of Commerce. Here's what happened: L.A. Mayor Richard Riordan, the Orange County Board of Supervisors and Disney CEO Michael Eisner called Buckingham Palace on September 9, 1997, and asked that the funeral for Princess Diana be transferred to Topanga Canyon. (Boy, did the Europeans steal the show with that one.) Our guys made a conference call to the Royal Family proposing that it would be better for humanity and the two boys if Diana were buried in Malibu rather than in Kensington, where they don't even have a theme park or anything.

"She was after all the 'people's princess'" Eisner pointed out, "and we have more people here in L.A. than you do. So how about it?"

Charles was for it, of course; especially since Gwyneth Paltrow and Brad had broken up. The Queen was certainly behind the concept. "Splendid idea," she says. "Diana so loved the surfing life." Philip was counting residuals. And the Arab guy that owns Harrods's—Dodi Fayed's dad—was talking to Eisner about a Princess Diana Funeral Parade that would replace the Parade of Lights that was doing so poorly at the park. All the ducks were lining up nicely when bam! Fate plants another stake into the cold, sad heart of Southern California hype. Bless her soul, Mother Teresa makes an untimely transition and Disney pulls out of the deal. "Sorry, just don't have room at the park for more than one parade."

I am sure at this point you are saying to yourself, yes, yes, William and Harry are dear to us (especially the one with the teeth like Diana's) but what about Lara? Sue? Is the Tupperware she bought last year doing the job? We love you—not for how cool you are or your proximity to the Mondrian Hotel—but for "who" you are as a people, as our favorite Christmas family. Please get to Lara's recitals, Sue's surgeries, and your own personal triumphs over flooring options and new wall coverings.

Ok. Ok. I'd better start with Sue. Her work this year with the felon population gives her an edge over my yard work stories.

True story: twenty felons are sitting around the day room of the Santa Ana Jail, pondering new tattoo ideas and watching playoff games from the seventies. Embezzlers, rapists, drug traffickers, murderers, lawyers; these are mean guys with a serious sense of personal space. The heavy metal doors of the jail open and Sue walks in like sunlight personified; wide-eyed, petite, with a demeanor more suited to Saks than the Santa Ana Jail. The doors bang shut with an echo that reaches all the way to Anaheim Stadium. She walks in front of these Latinos, Asians, Blacks, an East European and a white guy who was incarcerated as part of an affirmative action diversification program. Their eyes follow her in stark, incomprehensible wonder. What the hell is this? She stops in front of the television set, reaches up and turns it off. "Hey woman! Those are the Baltimore Colts you're messing with!"

"Hello," she says. "My name is Sue Mendizza and I would like to talk to you about your future."

"Look," she says. "You guys are entrepreneurs at heart. You had a dream and you followed it, even if it was stealing the retirement fund from your employer. The important thing is that you dreamed, you came up with a plan, you took action and then, unfortunately, you got caught. But now is not the time to give up, gentlemen. Now is the time to build your skill level so that next time…" They blink their eyes, trying to figure out whether the apparition standing before them is a con job or some kind of weird annunciation. They're all so mesmerized that they forget about the 1973 Colts game they'd just placed wagers on and they follow Sue like lemmings to computer class.

That's what Sue does most of the time: she dazes people, especially me, and then she hypnotizes them into doing what she wants them to do. Somehow, she always gets what she wants. Take deck week, for example.

We have this wooden patio deck in our backyard and the Irishman that put it in—you remember Joe, the guy that talks to leprechauns—anyway, before he finished our deck, Joe was touched by the spirit and became this passionate Christian evangelist staying up late at night at the local coffeehouse trying to convert all the yuppie kids that go to the local Catholic high school. That meant he totally lost interest in our deck. Instead of finishing it with a nice stain and sealer, I think he used napalm. It cracked and bubbled badly. I told Sue I was not going out there and sand the damn deck. No, no, no, no, no, no! I said. I am too busy. I don't have time to redo the deck. No. no, no, no, no, no!

July 12. Nine o'clock in the morning: I'm at Home Base asking a guy in an apron how to sand a deck.

As you recall, '96 was the Year of the Missing Shoe. Searching for Lara's shoes consumed as much time in our lives as work and sleep. I have designated 1997 The Year of Homework Ad Infinitum. Lara entered third grade back in September. She's in a class for gifted kids, and her teacher, Mr. Edmonds, feels that if any of his kids are not granted admission to M.I.T. by the end of the year, he has failed as an educator. In the beginning, parents were very upset with the amount of homework Mr. Edmonds was assigning. They picketed his classroom, reported him anonymously to the IRS, and lobbied the principle to give him the worst recess period. Mr. Edmonds defended himself by explaining that his kids had to begin thinking and planning their work a week ahead of time. "That's how they do it at M.I.T.," he explains.

"A week at a time!" screamed hysterical parents. "Our kids don't even know what day it is. How are they going to plan their work a week at time?" But Mr. Edmonds was patient and believe it or not, after a couple of months, even Lara was beginning to think ahead a little. In fact, thinking ahead wasn't really the biggest problem. The homework itself wasn't that hard, either; trig., Latin, seminars on Franz Kafka and particle physics, shit like that. The problem we had, and the reason I deemed this the year of Homework Ad Infinitum, is we couldn't seem to get even the shortest, simplest thing all the way done. We would get a good start on a reading passage with the five comprehension questions. But it was kind of like Zeno, the Greek philosopher, who pointed out the paradox of progress itself: that in order to get from point A to point B one would have to traverse half the distance between the two points, and then traverse half the remaining distance, and then half that distance. He concluded his argument by saying there were an infinite number of halves that had to be traversed so theoretically no one could really get from point A to point B. And that certainly turned out to be the case with Lara's homework. We could easily get half way, but to reach point B was impossible. Thus, Homework Ad Infinitum.

Like right now, she's sitting at her desk presumably working on a series of differential equations. I look over at her with pride, but am shocked to see that not one single unknown quantity has been identified. Instead, Lara has spilled all of my colored paper clips out onto the desk and is using them to create a replica of the NBC peacock. "Come on Lara, get to work," I say. And she does. But when I turn back a half an hour later thinking I am going see some nice scientific looking formulas worked out on her paper, I see instead a paper-clip sculpture of Gumby.

For Lara to actually complete any of her homework, I have to hover close by and become a nag, which of course is not something that comes natural to me.

While she is working, I try to find something that I can do, too, so I don't just waste my time. I start to add names and numbers to my Rolodex. This provides Lara with another opportunity to avoid her immediate task and fart around a little. "What are you doing?" she asks. "I'm updating my Rolodex," I respond.

"Want me to help?" "No," I say. "I want you to finish your cosmology." She draws some hair on a figure she calls "The Doctor of California." "Why are you doing that?" she asks. "I'm just trying to make some progress while I'm sitting here like a good parent trying to make you do your homework." "Progress?" she says, laughing like I was some kind of adult or something. "Progress? What's progress?"

So, her mind and mine work in a much different way. I'm logical. She's eight. I remember when we were driving back from a rehearsal for *Oliver*. While she was eating her In-N-Out burger—meat, cheese and ketchup, only; no lettuce, no tomato, nothing nutritious, please—I was trying to explain the primary points of the compass to her. "Out here in Southern California," I say, "when you're driving toward the mountains or the hills you're usually headed east. When you're headed that way, to the ocean, you're usually headed west." Lara nods, her mouth full. She points and mumbles, "So east, west, south and north." "That's exactly correct," I say, proud of myself for providing such efficacious instruction. I take another step with her education by pointing out, "The sun always comes up over the mountains, too, sweetheart." Then I pose a question to test her comprehension. "So if the sun comes up over the mountains it comes up in the . . .?" I pause in order for Lara to fill in the blank with the correct answer. I wait, hopefully. She's chewing some fries. I get nothing. So I repeat, "The sun comes up in the . . ." Lara swallows, and says, "Morning.

On Saturdays we let Lara get up early and watch mindless cartoons on TV. We know it's bad for her brain development. We hate it. But just as we feel the need to expose her to cultured things like the $1.5 billion Starbucks they call the Getty Museum, we also feel that to forbid all TV would be a form of cultural depravation; I mean TV is our culture.

So she watches cartoons on Saturday morning just like my brother and I did back when we thought of Beanie and Cecil as superheroes. Lara is wrapped up in her blanket on the couch and I'm in the other room trying to be a role model for her by pretending to read Geoffrey Chaucer. After my second espresso, the jabbering from the television interrupts my concentration—just when I was getting to the good part—and I walk into the family room in a mature rage, "God I hate these cartoons. All the characters do is squeal, screech and squeak in those totally phony and contrived voices. Can't any of them just speak in a normal tone?"

Lara doesn't even know I'm there, or at least she doesn't let on that she knows. She is quite used to these mature, well-conceived tantrums. "Listen to them! Squaakk! Screeeech! Squeeeeek! Squaakk! Screeech! Squeeeek!" I say reasonably. Finally, she's had enough. She doesn't remove her eyes from the TV screen, but she does move her head a little in my direction and with a dismissive calm says, "They're mice, Dad. Mice squeak!"

Back in June, Lara performed a small role in the musical, *Oliver*. It was a pretty amazing experience for our entire family. The production was staged by a big professional theater group in Irvine with a bunch of very talented principle actors, musicians and choreographers. Lara was a small part of a very large chorus of kids, but we thought it would be a good experience for her to see all the different parts of a musical get fleshed out in rehearsal and then staged. In order to stay close to Lara and make sure no directors tried to sign her up without our lawyer looking at the contract, Sue and I volunteered as stagehands, and that was interesting, too. Lara was singing *Oliver* tunes for weeks during rehearsals. I was singing them, too; in the car, the shower, during important meetings with clients. The music was infectious.

Finally, on opening night, she got to sing on stage. I was an usher toward the back of the house, doing nothing much more than thinking about my daughter backstage, getting on her pauper costume, preparing herself, playing with the rest of the kids. I still worry about her. Is she nervous? Are these people being kind to her? Is she getting lost in the crowd? I'd better go down to the dressing room and check on her one more time.

But the house lights suddenly go down. The audience settles into whispers. The music begins. Stage lights come on. From each far aisle of the theater hundreds of kids dressed as orphans begin marching in time down the steps toward the stage, each one carrying a little bowl into which they will later place their meager portion of gruel. Suddenly, the children burst out singing this touching song called "Food." Their uneven, but thoroughly angelic voices fill the theater and we, the audience, are stunned to silence. The song is sweet and funny, but very sad, too; because they're singing about something they need badly, but don't have.

Food, glorious food!
Don't care what it looks like.
Burned, underdone or crude.
Don't care what the cooks like.
Just thinking of growing fat.
Our senses are reeling.
One moment of knowing that
Full up feeling.
Food, glorious food!

Although I had been working with the cast for several weeks, I was not prepared for the feelings that surfaced. My chest relaxed. Tears came to my eyes and I just felt like crying up there in the dark. Seeing and hearing these kids sing in such dear, imperfect concert as they marched in step toward the stage was more beautiful than Mozart, sunsets or even a good playoff game. They marched down to the stage, hundreds of them, where they formed a precious children's chorus for the conclusion. "Food! Glorious Food!" I was crying at the end of the number. First, because it was very moving theater. Because my daughter was in the show, which in a way meant that she had grown some; grown up, grown a bit away from me, and grown deeper into the complicated world of her time and society. We are a dear, precious people, we humans, and so all the sadder that a story like *Oliver Twist* could ever have been conceived and written, that the raw material for such a story could even exist. So there I was, tough guy of the western world, weeping up there in the dark for myself and my daughter and my world, as Lara sang her first song on stage. After the show, we went over to In-N-Out for meat and cheese on a bun, a modest cuisine I think even poor Oliver may have refused. Like, "I said, food please. This isn't food."

OK, now is a good time to set down the letter and take a break. You deserve it. You've done well. Maybe you should go to work for a while, or turn on a playoff game. For newcomers, let me review my philosophy of Christmas epistles. Like Kant and Jacques Derrida, I believe that a family worth writing a Christmas letter about deserves more than just hitting the highlights of the year; like Jimmy learned to swim; Tammy's in ballet; Kenneth's wearing dresses. I mean it changes everything when you learn that Jimmy is 26. Details make all the difference, which brings me to Tahoe, our first real family vacation.

We were supposed to be on the road by noon on Friday the 8th of November, but Eisenhower was supposed to have been in Normandy on September 4, too. Did he make it? No. Why?

Cause his guys couldn't find their other boot, that's why. Could we expect more from our little girl? Sue of course was frazzled from trying to get all those felons into grad school before we departed. Henry, our new landscape artist, was outside redoing all the landscape that we did last year, moving the birch tree out of the sun and the palms into it. "How much," I asked. He laughed. "More than last year?" Laugh. "Yeah, that's what I figured." Sue's Mom was in the kitchen meticulously packing healthy food into Lara's lunchbox as Sue and I loaded the cooler with Ding Dongs and high-fructose soft drinks to counter any impact that real food might have on Lara. We loaded the trunk, threw in an extra shoe, picked Lara up from school, dropped a big check off at my accountant's to ward off the state, and then—free at last—we drove up the ramp of the 55 freeway, where we quickly came to a complete stop. Gridlock. I turn to Sue and say, "Friday." She turn's to me and says, "Four o'clock." We stare at each other and simultaneously find ourselves saying, "Veterans' Day?"

Like D-day, it was a little slow in the beginning, but we had a nice drive north to Lake Tahoe, and the first thing we did when we woke in the morning was go horseback riding; or at least Lara and I did. We were greeted at the stables by Bob the Cowboy. Later, Harriet and her two daughters, Amy and Brook, joined us for the ride. We rode single file up the cold mountain trail to the top where we got a breathtaking view of the lake, surrounded by the gray chiseled sentries of the High Sierras. On the way down, I started to sing "My Darling Clementine," rocking back and forth to the rhythm of my trusty steed, Arnold. Lara turned red with shame. She pounded her heels into the sides of her horse and bolted toward the head of the line where Cowboy Bob was leading us through the snow-dusted wilderness. "He's not my real father," she says to Bob. Bob nodded and said, "Most kids bring fake parents on these rides." But it didn't bother me. I just kept on singing. In a way I figured it was good for Lara to get used to me embarrassing her in front of strangers. I mean this is just the beginning, sweetheart.

The great thing about being in Tahoe in November is that it snows, and then it clears up and the sun comes out, and then it snows again. When the weather broke, Lara, Sue and I took a chance and looked for a good place to hike. We scanned the map together and decided on Eagle Falls, not too far outside of Tahoe City.

We drove to the trailhead. The sun was still out and the snow-capped mountains and tall pines and rugged volcanic terrain shimmered in the morning light. On our way up the trail, we came to a sign that said, Desolation Wilderness, which I thought added to the adventure. We kept climbing and as we did the surroundings became more and more natural, quieter, less human. With the light snowfall, the trail itself became a little difficult to follow and I showed Lara how to build markers that would help us find our way back in the event that we couldn't locate the trail. I told her that I was part Indian and my ancestors taught me these things in my dreams.

We walked uphill in the beautiful forest for about an hour when suddenly, as we climbed up over a large granite rock formation, we saw this little alpine lake all by itself, sunk into the mountain like a precious gemstone. It was stunning to behold, the still blue water with a little ribbon of sunlight shimmering from the far shore, to the one closest to us, like being touched by something that seems very much beyond us and yet, at the same time, right there in front of our eyes. There wasn't another person around, just Sue and Lara and me. We sat there for a moment, a little in awe of what we had found, and amazed that we were the only ones there, so silent and fresh was this placid lake, and so full of meaning. Then Lara said, "Follow me," and we began to explore the area. Sue stayed behind. She was either in a deep profound state of meditation, or trying to decide between Italian and Thai for lunch; I'm never sure. It was a special time at the lake, at least for me; special for two reasons, because of the beauty and because the three of us were able to share it together.

The casinos that lined the shoreline at the southern end of the lake were a stark contrast to the pristine natural beauty around it. We go to Harrah's and even though it was pretty dingy and tacky, we had some fun, mostly because every time Sue put a coin into a slot machine, lights started to blink off and on, bells rang, and money dropped out. She couldn't lose. It got to the point where she would just walk down a row of slots dropping a coin in each machine and Lara and I would follow behind her with one of those plastic cups in each hand, catching her winnings as they flowed out like manna. Eventually the gangsters who run the casino politely walked up to us and told us that kids were not allowed on the gambling floor. We played dumb (which isn't hard for us). Huh? No kids? Huh? "Yes, sir," said the gangster. "Our adult clientele don't like children to see what ignorant, besotted fools they are."

We stayed in Tahoe until the college fund was completely exhausted and then we drove across the state to Carmel where we stayed a couple of nights. While playing tennis with Lara, I tore the tendons in my ankle and spent the trip home riding shotgun with an ice pack on my leg, whining about how miserable life can be. In between groans, we talked about the death of Princess Diana.

I argued that it was just one more attempt by the European community to draw attention away from L.A. "The poor woman just got a lot more attention than I think she deserved," I said. "She was a symbol for the world," countered Sue. I said a lot of women have accomplished more than Diana, but haven't received near the attention. "Like who?" Sue responds. And I'm thinking major opportunity here for marital points: "You, sweetheart."

Ok. Sue's not perfect. She puts open cans of Pepsi back into the refrigerator. Last week we caught her listening to a Skeeter Davis recording. But aside from a few things like that, Sue is an aristocracy of one, both regal and real, unlike most of those monarchs. In fact I know a lot of women who deserve a week's worth of media coverage for the contributions they have made to our lives: Cindy, Cheryl, Kay, Marsha, Betty, Bonnie, Edna, Lilo, Peggy, Merry, Jan, Mercedes, Sunji, Diane, Anita, Elsa, Lucille, Ann, Tedra, Sara, Bessie, Carolyn, Maggie, Maria, Dorothy, Donna, Farida, Margarita, Debbie, Monica, Judith, Kathryn, Robyn, Linda, Hede, Eiko, Rosine, Christina, Stacy, Hillary, Sara, Joanne, Patti, Karen, Bobbe, Penina, Darlyne . . and the list goes on.

Face it, it is we (or us), the people of mortgages and the norm, who make "cool" people possible in the world. Only against the background of the common man and woman are exceptions like Gwyneth Paltrow and Brad Pitt even allowed to exist, a fact rarely understood by historians, deconstructionists or Hollywood screenwriters. Bottom line, without our lives, they're lives would be just like ours. (If anyone understands what I just said, would you please give me a call.)

Back home, I was walking around our own little lake with Lara when out of nowhere she said to me, "Sometimes it just feels so weird to be alive. Sometimes it just comes over me and I feel so weird to be alive. Sometimes I will try and feel this way, but I can't. And then sometimes it just happens. I'm not sure if it's OK to tell anyone. Usually I wouldn't tell anyone." And I say, "You can tell me anything, sweetheart. Usually you're just too busy doing stuff and you don't realize you're actually alive. But sometimes you catch a glimpse of yourself being alive and that is very weird." "Yeah," she says.

And as we begin the final stretch to the year 2000, I think that is what Sue and Lara and I would hope for all of our friends, both here and abroad: that you catch yourselves "being alive" a lot more often in '98 than you did last year. To us, your lives are absolutely precious, and next to being on TV, "feeling alive" is probably the coolest thing that can happen.

Stay hip, and have a great year!

With our Love,

Mark, Sue, Lara & Fergie

"The hippest story in the world is the one taking place at your breakfast table."

—Aristotle 454 B.C

1997
Important Events

- **Dow hits 7000.**

  Now it really is too high!

- **E-bay becomes site of choice for Internet sellers and buyers.**

  Sue becomes expert at "logging on."

- **First mammal (a sheep) is cloned in Scotland. They name her Dolly.**

  Lara finishes a homework assignment on time!

- **NASA's Pathfinder spacecraft lands on Mars and the rover, Sojourner, begins to explore the planet for signs of life.**

  Lara looks for signs of life in Mom and Dad.

- **Brad Pitt and Gwyneth Paltrow break up.**

  Nobody seems to care, including Gwyneth.

- **Dow hits 8000.**

  "Are you kidding ME?"

The Year of Betty and Veronica

Mark, Sue, Lara and Fergie
Orange County, California

Christmas 1998

Hi Everyone,

It's us, again, but this will have to be quick. Menorahs are already aflame, Ramadan starts in a couple of days–right after the bombing stops–and Christmas is looming. Must be brief, then: twenty pages, max!

First, a report on the goals I set for myself this year: I didn't achieve a single one. Zip! Remember, I had three. I was going to find the zone, enter the zone, and get on TV. I wrote out the goals just like it said in the book to do. But before I had a chance to work up an action plan, the year was over. I went back to the book to see what it said about failure to achieve a goal and I was very pleased to find that it doesn't really matter. The book says that one can always modify one's goals. Don't feel guilty, it says. Be realistic. And so this year I'm doing just that. I'm ratcheting down my expectations. I'm still going to look for the zone. And when I find it, I'm still going to enter and remain for as long as I can inside the zone. But I'm changing my goal about getting on TV to just getting up in the morning and getting my shorts on right.

We are taking action as a family, however, to make more time for ourselves. We're going to Cancun. As you know, the ancient and mysterious Mayan civilization existed down there on the Yucatan peninsula for over 800 years. During that time they never figured out how to make steel or a wheel or zippers, but they did create an extraordinary calendar based on precise observations of the solar system and a new technique for rounding numbers. The net result is a calendar with a lot more time on it than we have up here.

The Mayan work week, for example, started and finished on the same day. I mean it was like the Mayan work "day." The rest of the week, which was more like two or three weeks depending on how you rounded off the numbers, they spent working on their goals and sacrificing young female children to the gods. We're going down there in January to get one of those calendars. It should give us a lot more time this year.

We also want to show Lara what it's like to live in another culture. We booked a week at the luxurious Cancun Hyatt Hotel Resort and authentic Mayan Village, where we hope she will learn more about room service and how to communicate effectively with a concierge. She already knows how to say, "Can you get me a limo, please?" and "Who's the manager around here?" But there's no substitute for actually living in a different culture, and by the time we get home we hope she will be able to negotiate upgrades and late checkout. That's our goal, anyway.

Usually, I try to summarize for our friends abroad the noteworthy events that have taken place here in Southern California during the last year. Not in '98, though. Nothing has happened in SoCal this year, or last. In fact, nothing has happened since O.J. We used to have riots and earthquakes and massive fires and floods that caused people to embrace the lord and inventory their possessions. But not anymore. These days the cool things are all happening in Washington, Baghdad and the Johnson

Space Center. Southern California is completely off the "happening" scope. In fact the only thing that is of much interest here happened today. Christmas trees have begun bursting into flames like some kind of spontaneous combustion or something. Could be the heat. I mean the high in Orange County today was about 102 degrees, and it's December 17. I'm driving down the 405 freeway toward South Coast Plaza to buy Sue some new fine bone china. We're still eating out of the mess kits I got when I was discharged from the Navy Seals, and one of the things I promised Sue when we got married was that she would have some of the finest things in the world, like furniture and plates. The mess kits work for me, but apparently you can't put those little pans in the microwave. So I'm heading north on the San Diego freeway with Villeroy & Boch dancing like sugar plums in my head when I see this little red Renault in front of me. There's a Christmas tree tied onto the roof, and it's sort of fluttering in the draft like a big-eared dog with its head out the window. Suddenly, the tree just burst into flames. I've seen that happen to men in staff meetings before, but never to a tree. Here's where that horsepower I paid an extra $15,000 for when I bought the Beamer comes in handy. Pedal to the floor, I pull up next to the Renault and point to his roof. "Hey buddy, your tree's on fire!" The guy looks up and then rolls his eyes. "Damn it," he yells back. "That's the third tree today!"

By the time I got to South Coast Plaza I'd seen no fewer than ten Christmas trees in flames on the top of vehicles on the 405. And apparently it was happening all over Southern California. Unseasonably high temperatures? Perhaps. Global warming? Maybe. My theory is that the high stress that we all experience during the holidays reached combustible levels. My brother, who moved out of Southern California this year to live in a tent with his family in the foothills of the Sierra Nevadas, is always telling me that the vibrations of the human heart can be felt for several miles away. If that's true, and I am sure it is if Mike says so, then I figure the vibrations of extreme gift anxiety could easily set a tree on fire. Aside from what Sue and Lara and I have been doing with our lives (like the bone china, for example, and Lara's report on the Spanish explorer, Cortez), the exploding Christmas Tree Mystery is the only thing that's happened in Southern California this year that's worth mentioning.

Sue has had an especially exciting and successful year, both professionally and personally. Professionally she got another raise, and personally she spent it. When she's not transforming prison inmates into Arthurian knights, she works on her new hobby: painting. Yes. Sue's become an artist. She and I went shopping back in the springtime for some original artwork for our home. We said to ourselves, no more lithos. No more serigraphs. No more of those landscape paintings they sell in front of the grocery store. We visited several galleries and saw some things that we liked, but after looking at the price tags we figured we could paint our own originals and probably enjoy them just as much as we would a painting from some stranger living next to Carly Simon in Martha's Vineyard. So I bought Sue a big canvas and some oils and I said, "Paint!"

Boy! What a surprise. Sue and Lara sat down one Saturday afternoon and in the course of about three hours splattered paint over the canvas in such a unique and surprisingly masterful way that by the time Sue was finished we had ourselves a genuine work of art, as good as anything I had seen at Leo Castelli's or Mary Boone's, better in fact, since Sue was the painter. At first she wanted to paint butterflies against a bright sunny field with a border of happy faces, but I objected to that as being too self-indulgent. "Where's your darker side?" I asked. She says she doesn't have a darker side. I say everybody has a darker side. And she says OK, she'll leave out the happy faces. I say go a bit deeper. "How deep?" she asks. I say what about something that represents the beginnings of human consciousness. Fine, she says.

And she begins. At first, her painting was a strange gestural tone poem of dark earthen hues that merged with incalculable subtlety into nascent reds and oranges. This was because we could only afford a few tubes of paint—anybody price oil paints lately? Geeez! She had a limited palette to work with, but what she achieved was breathtaking. As the painting developed, it was as if the origins of human consciousness had been gradually transformed into this uncontrollable conflagration of passionate emotions that threatened to escalate and overpower the very consciousness that had given birth to the feelings in the first place, a kind of Mary Poppins meets the cave painters of Lascaux, if you know what I mean.

Thus, in 1998 the Suist Manifesto was born. Suism states that true art can only come from an artist who is totally uncompromised by training, talent or paint. And a true Suist only paints one painting. None of that blue period and red period and all that bullshit. You paint one, and then get on with your life. Today, there are Suists following in Sue's footsteps all over the world and their singular good work is showing up in some of the finest galleries in the world. But make no mistake: we have the original Suist, as well as Sue herself, right here in our house. Felons from Sue's jail stand guard over the piece, and it is truly something to behold.

I'm going to deem 1998 the "Year of Betty and Veronica." It's an Archie comic book written from the female point of view, and Lara has been reading them one after another. At first I was shocked that she found it so absorbing. "I thought you were reading the Milton I bought for you sweetheart." "Satan scared me," she responds. I tell her that I used to read Archie comics all the time and she finds that amusing. "Archie has a problem with commitment, doesn't he?" I ask. "What's commitment?" she inquires without taking her eye off the comic. "It's like when you give up one thing that you want real bad so that you can have another thing that you also want real bad." "Why can't you just have both?" she asks. "Yeah. I think that's how Archie sees it," I respond. For over fifty years, Betty and Veronica have been vying for his affections and they're still at it. Still in high school, too.

And so this was the year in which popular culture began to slowly insinuate itself into Lara's inner selves. She discovered the Spice Girls this year, Betty and Veronica, and of course Bill Clinton. I walk by Lara's room on Saturday afternoon and she and Chelsea are in there singing loudly to the Spice Girls CD. I say to Sue, "She's a teenager. She's not even nine and she's turned into a teenager already. I mean in one day she became a teenager. How did that happen?"

Another thing that has struck me, and added to the many things that make me anxious about being a parent, is the existence of gender bias in the world Lara is gradually entering. I suppose it's inevitable, since girls and boys are so different. There are naturally going to be different perceptions and standards. And I want Lara to be feminine, whatever that means. But I'm very wary of the bias in favor of boys in so many areas of our lives, like the selection of middle linebackers, for example.

Lara and I are outside playing catch while we wait for Stacy to drive up and take the kids to school. Lara says, "Dad, have any girls ever played on the Angels, or the Dodgers, or the Indians?" I have to say no. "Those are professional teams. The men on those teams play for money. Girls generally do not play on baseball teams for money. A lot of girls play baseball, but not too many play for money." I'm uncomfortable. I don't know quite how to put this. It's pretty clear that Lara is beginning to see that it's the men who gain celebrity in high visibility professional sports like baseball, football and basketball. I try to explain. "See, boys are generally bigger and stronger than girls." "Except for Katie," she says. "Well, yes, in third grade there's not that much difference between boys and girls." "Like Walker is tall," she says, "but he's skinny and Katie is stronger than he is." "Yes," I say, "not all guys are stronger than all girls, that's not what I meant. But . . ." See? I have to work this out.

And then once while we were at the pool Lara raised the question of gender preference, again. It was a hot Sunday afternoon. Sue, Lara and I had been playing tennis. After I beat everyone, we decided to go swimming in the pool, but we had forgotten our bathing suits. So Sue drove home to get them and Lara and I sat under the big umbrella and watched the sparsely populated pool. It was mostly filled with boys and their fathers. Erratic, edgy little boys and muscular men seeking a very narrow range of satisfaction through the infliction of pain upon their aquatic comrades. They were shooting each other in the face with water guns. Hitting each other over the head with inflatable clubs. Grabbing each other in strangleholds and making what appeared to be earnest attempts at drowning one another. This and other unrestrained and equally aberrant fantasies all acted out in the blinding blue reflection of chlorinated water while Lara sat under the umbrella and watched.

"Did you want a girl or a boy?" she asks. Without hesitating I say, "A girl. A girl for sure." "Why?" she continues. I don't want to be too hard on my gender, so I say, "Because boys are so aggressive and stupid and mean." "Well," she says, "would you want to be a girl?" And I have to pause a little. If I say yes, am I gay? If I say no, what will it do to Lara's self-image? I think to myself, how would Bill Clinton parse this question? ("It depends on what you mean by the word girl.) "No," I say. "I'm kind of used to being a guy. But I definitely wanted a girl." Lara says, "Katie wants to be a boy." "Why does she want to be a boy?" "Because they can play baseball and basketball." "But girls can play baseball and basketball." "I know. I play basketball all the time. But she says she wants to be half-girl and half-boy." And I say, "Look honey, who does most of the crime in the world?" Lara thinks and says, "Boys." "And who starts wars?" She thinks and says, "Boys." And who hurts the most people in the world? She says, "Boys." And then she says, "I'll say that to Katie the next time she says she wants to be a boy." Then there's a long pause, and she says, "I think I want to ride in the back of a truck again." And I go, "Huh?"

Lara and I read *Alice's Adventures in Wonderland* and *Alice Through the Looking Glass.* Each night for a long time we just lay together in bed and read these two utterly upside-down, irrational tales. Whoever you are. Wherever you live. Find these books and read them to your kids. It's like being in the same dream together, an automatic and eternal bond.

Here's a school success story: call it Lara and Goliath. Lara and Sue had worked hard to prepare for Lara's math test. It was a comprehensive test of seventy questions that covered the material students were to master throughout the year. Her teacher, Mr. Edmunds, required an 85% to pass. I picked Lara up from school on the day she finished taking the exam. As we walked toward the car, I took her heavy backpack off her slender shoulder. "Let me carry that," I said. We got into the car; Lara in the back;

me, like her chauffeur, in the front, and headed to the bagel shop where we get our after-school snack. "Well, did you pass your test?" I asked. "No," she said. "I missed it by one point." I am truly ashamed to say that I was really upset. This is not the place in Lara's development to be obsessing about a grade. I hide my perverse parental reaction. "Oh well, you can take it again," I say as I pulled into the parking stall at the bagel place.

Later, at home, I took a look at the test and realized, again to my disappointment, that she really had grasped all the mathematical concepts. She knew quite well how to solve all the problems, but forgot to check her answers. She left out a dollar sign here, forgot to label an answer there, all simple careless errors. I gave her a big hug and said, "You know, you are great at math. You have really mastered it this year. But you're terrible at taking tests." I told her I was very proud of her.

As I scrutinized the test a little further, however, I saw one item that troubled me. There was a picture of a quarter, a dime, a nickel and penny on the page. The instructions said, "What is the value of the coins?" Lara wrote down the number 25 cents, ten cents, five cents and one cent, which to me was correct. "What's wrong with this one?" I asked.

Apparently. there are similar problems in their book with a slightly different wording, something like, "What is the value of each group of coins?" This wording of course asked the student to add up the different values of the coins and render a sum. But the item on the test did not ask that question. Sue went and got the math book and we confirmed our suspicions. This item was not the same as the items in the book. Lara had followed the instructions and had arrived at the correct answer and yet it was marked wrong.

The item made the difference between passing the test and

not passing. The three of us were sitting there at the foot of the stairs, staring down at the math problem and pondering our next course of action.

Lara wanted to take the test again, because I promised her if she got an A in math I wouldn't walk outside in my underwear anymore. But it didn't seem right to me to just allow this mistake on the part of Mr. Edmunds to remain unchallenged. "Don't you think we should tell Mr. Edmunds about this?" I asked Lara. She became very apprehensive and said; "Mr. Edmunds does not like to be corrected." And it's true. He's a very nice guy, and a great teacher, but the kids are afraid to walk up and ask him questions because his tendency is to respond to them with a challenge; "Have you looked in the book?" "Were you listening when I explained that in class?" "What are you, some kind of loser?"

So it is not surprising that Lara would be apprehensive about walking up to the teacher and claiming that he made a mistake when grading her test. "Can't you talk to him?" she asked me. I was tempted, but resisted. "No, honey. You can do it. Just walk up and point to this problem and say you feel this one is correct. You can do that." We actually rehearsed what she was going to say. Just say, "The item on the test instructs us to find the value of the coins. The problem in the book asks us to find the value of the group of coins. That makes a difference and I think I did this correctly."

Lara repeated this over and over in the car on the way to school.

Later in the day, Sue came up to me with tears in her eyes and said the most amazing thing happened today. What happened, I asked. "Lara walked up to Mr. Edmonds and confronted him about the math problem," she explained weepily. "He said he agreed with her completely. He not only changed her grade to

86%, but he told her that she was the only one in class who was brave enough to come up to the mean old teacher and challenge him. But don't tell her I told you."

I left the house to do errands and stuff, but made a point of buying Lara a yacht and some pool toys. I arrived home later that night, about nine o'clock, just before Lara was ready to go to bed. She ran down the stairs to meet me. She was bursting with excitement and enthusiasm. "Guess what, Daddy . . ." And she told me again what had happened. She said that Jessica was sharpening her pencil close by Mr. Edmond's desk when she walked up and told Mr. Edmonds that he had made a mistake. "Jessica's jaw dropped open," she said. "She couldn't believe I was telling Mr. Edmonds he had made a mistake." It was an important lesson for her because she is by nature shy with adults, and even more so when they possess as much authority and power over her life as a third-grade teacher. I think she learned that if one has a good case, one can challenge any authority figure, unless they're like your boss or something.

When we sold our blue Volvo this year, Lara broke down and wept. It caught Sue and me off guard. What's the matter honey? We don't use the Volvo anymore sweetheart and we need to get our $5,000. But her heart was broken and inconsolable. We'd had the Volvo ever since Lara was born and it was unthinkable to her that we could just sell it to some stranger. "I don't care about the money," she cried. "I want the Volvo back." It took days to get over, and it wasn't until I had proven that we had found a nice home with a loving family who would take care of the car that we were able to go on with our lives.

As the Volvo incident pointed out, most kids are much more sensitive than we adults can even know. In fact I think most kids are clairvoyant, until we numb them down with standards for grade-level and SAT preparation. I was getting Lara ready for bed one night when she said, "Dad, can I tell you something?" I climbed up and lay at the foot of her bed. "You know, sometimes I imagine things and then the things I imagine happen exactly like I imagined they would." I listened. "Like tonight?" I asked. We had dinner with my sister, and Lara told me that she saw the whole thing in her mind's eye months ago. "Aunt Marsha said exactly the things that I imagined she would say. She made the exact same movements that I imagined. It was like I was in a dream." When did you imagine this? Months ago, she says. "I imagine these things months before they happen. And then when they are happening I feel like I am remembering them." "That's very special sweetheart. I want you to pay attention to that. It may be a gift that we can exploit for money someday." And she said, "I don't want this gift. I want to fly."

Lara saw a bear this year up in Washington. She and Sue and Bill and Marilyn were up there to watch Bill perform in an outdoor theater production of *The Sound of Music.* The theater is in the woods. Before the show they all went for a walk. Bill said, "If you see a bear, whatever you do don't panic and don't run." As they walked along, they heard a rustling behind the bushes. They all froze. "It's the bear," says Bill. "Freeze!" Sue grabs Lara and runs like a son of a bitch back down the hill.

Yes, I am whitening my teeth with that peroxide solution. Now I'll be like the rest of the boomers whose faces resemble a lava flow, while their brilliant white teeth look like something from Tiffany's.

I read a book which says there are really only four big things left for scientists to discover: quantum gravity, the causes of human consciousness, how life began, and one more. I think it was finding out where the lids to Tupperware go.

Lara and I campaigned hard this year for the election of Tom Wilson as Orange County Supervisor for the second district. Tom doesn't want to see the quality of life in Orange County become what it is in Los Angeles, and so he is against the airport that is proposed for El Toro. In our opinion, the vision that the airport people have for us is basically let's be like L.A. and build out every open space we can get our hands on. The airport is symbolic of the nineteenth century thinking that is still so prevalent on County Boards of Supervisors and city governments. I call it the open space half-life phenomenon. "Hey," says the nice builder, "We're only going to take half the open space." Then the next builder comes and says, "Look, we're only going to take half of what the last builder left." And then the next incarnation comes along and takes half of that space. And by the time Lara can vote, there really won't be anything left to vote for; nothing really left to fight for. South Orange County won't be any different from Inglewood. Of course, the builders and retired politicians will all be living in Maui.

Sue and Lara and I were invited to the big rally to watch the results come in, and I must say, it was pretty wild. It's strange how really childish adult men and women can become when they're fighting hard for what they believe in. Tom won, and remained pretty dignified.

In addition to witnessing one of Lara's most extraordinary years of growth and achievement, we also caught her in her first lie. "Did you take all your vitamins this morning?" asked Sue. "Yes," answered Lara. "Honest?" "Yes." "Are you telling me the truth?" "Yes."

Sue had been asking Lara this question for more than a week, receiving the same affirmative answers. Yes, I took all my vitamins just like you told me. One day, however, Sue decided to count the vitamins in the bottle. It had apparently been a full bottle when she gave it to Lara and after one week, it had apparently remained a full bottle. Uh, Oh! Lara had blown it. And Sue was very distressed. When she came into the bathroom and told me that Lara had been lying about her vitamins, I laughed. But Sue didn't think it was funny. She said we have to "ground" her. I laughed at that, too because we had never grounded Lara for anything in her life.

Sue's proposition just sounded unreal to me. But she was adamant. "We have to punish her this time," she said. "But when I want to punish her," I whined, "you always say that I'm being too hard on her. Now that you want to punish her, it's all of a sudden this very serious matter." "Ellen says if we don't stop this thing now, it will really be a problem later on, especially when she becomes a teenager. She'll be taking drugs and lying about it and it will be totally out of control." "So fine," I said "Let's ground her." Sue said, "I told her that she can't play with Chelsea for a week."

Later I go down stairs and find Lara sitting on the white couch in the living room, a little weepy. I hold her in my arms. "You and me and mommy have to tell each other the truth," I say like Gregory Peck in "To Kill a Mockingbird." "Otherwise we won't be able to trust each other. And we have to trust each other. People lie sometimes. Not everyone tells the truth all the time, but it's very important that you and me and mommy tell each other the truth. Do you understand?" Lara nods in contrition. There's a pause. She sniffles. And then says, "So, is there a Santa Claus?"

The next morning is the final rehearsal for *The Sound of Music* before opening night. Sue and I have been taking the girls back and forth to rehearsal all week. Sue's in bed with the stomach flu.

It's very early. And very cold. Lara is in costume, dressed in a beautiful white wedding gown. We're both shivering. She gets in the back seat, while I try to get the damn controls on the heater in the BMW to work. I'm stressed, not just about rehearsals, but about all the other things I have to get done that day. Why can't they just have a pipe run by the manifold like they did in the old Volvo? Computerized heaters never work.

I stop to pick up Lara's friend, Kathryn. It's about six thirty in the morning and Kathryn comes out in the wedding gown that she will wear in the play. "Don't you have a sweater, sweetheart?" "No," she says. I get angry at her parents for letting Kathryn come out in the cold without a jacket. She gets in the back seat with Lara. Both of them are in stunning new white wedding gowns, and they are both very proud. Anticipation is building, some apprehension, too. But mostly they are both just totally excited about being on stage with their friends in their new gowns, their beautiful white gowns.

I drop the kids off at the theater. I get a coffee and a bagel and drive back home, tired. Organizing the day in my mind. Making a few calls on the cell phone.

Two hours later, I'm back at my desk when disaster hits. I receive a call from a woman at the theater who tells me that Lara has become very ill and is throwing up. My lungs contract. My heart sinks. In her new wedding dress. "I'll be right down."

Sue's in bed, still sick. "Lara is throwing up all over the place," I say. "I'm going to get her." I am so sad. This was her big day. How must she feel? This is the hardest part of parenting, this increasingly frequent feeling of helplessness. I listen to the radio on the way down. The Pope is landing in Cuba for the first time ever, but there's hardly any news coverage. It's all Bill Clinton, Ken Starr and Republicans with their sordid little coup.

A bad day for me and the nation.

I park in the handicap space and walk quickly to the rear door to the theater. As I approach the entrance, I see a blonde woman sitting on a bench next to the door. She is wearing black slacks and a black sweater and looks Diane Sawyerish. There is a large bundle on her lap, covered with a blanket. I walk past, open the door and walk inside. "May I help you," asks the woman as if I am intruding. I hate these people who substitute the authority of a clerk for kindness and a real life. "My name is Mark Mendizza," I say. "Someone called and told me my daughter was ill." She changes her tone completely and walks me back towards the door where the blonde woman is sitting with the big bundle on her lap.

The bundle of course is my daughter, Lara. I pull back the blanket and there she is—pale, pale Lara. The woman gently removes the cover from Lara's shoulder. I kneel and place my hand on her forehead. "Are you sick, honey? You got the bug that mommy has, didn't you?" The women says, "She shouldn't be left alone in a corner, somewhere. If my daughter were sick, I would want someone to hold her." And I almost break down and cry. I am so grateful to this mom for holding Lara all this time, just sitting on the bench in front of the door holding my daughter in her arms, rocking her back and forth, until her father or mother could come and pick her up. There were probably 150 kids in this production. Yet this mom, whoever she was, stepped outside of the chaos, kneeled down and lifted up my sick little girl and held her for an hour and half. Jesus, thank you. "Thank you so much," I say to the woman. "It could be nerves, or it could be the flu," she says. And she hands me a paper sack which contains Lara's beautiful wedding dress, the costume she was so thrilled to wear on stage. She says, "I would have wanted someone to hold my daughter if she were ill."

Oh, thank you, thank you, thank you. I know those Germans can't help it if they have to computerize everything, even the damn heater. Doesn't matter. Kathryn's parents are doing the best they can. Clinton don't matter. Starr don't matter. Pope don't even matter. Not now. Not today. What matters today is that my most precious friend and daughter was helped by a stranger and I am so grateful. Instead of leaving her in a cold theater chair or by herself in a cot in the corner, this wonderful woman-mom held her in her arms. And that's our Christmas wish this year for all our friends and family: May your loved ones be cared for by people you don't even know. Yeah! I like that. Let's all do that, then: just care for each other this Christmas. Deeply care. All the way till say, New Year's! Then if we like it, we can go on 'til, like, February or March. And yes, darling: There is a Santa Claus. Absolutely. Totally. No lie.

With our caring love,

Fergie, Sue, Mark & Lara

1998
Important Events

- **President Clinton submits the first balanced budget in nearly three decades.**

  "Yeah, sure, but does it cover dance class and math tutors?

- **President Clinton is impeached along strictly partisan lines.**

  Lara suspects something fishy is going on with adults in her world.

- **Leaders in Northern Ireland reach peace accord.**

  Lara asks why it took 800 years. She sees a bear.

- **At 75 years old, John Glenn returns to space.**

  At 51, Mark considers switching careers and becoming an astronaut.

- **FDA approves Viagra. 10,000 prescriptions a day are written.**

  Sue is hopeful.

- **Dow hits 9000.**

  Mark crossing fingers for market crash.

The Year the Millennium Ended

Mark, Sue, Lara and Fergie
Orange County, California

December 20, 1999

Dear Friends, Family and Militia Members,

You may be glad to hear that this Christmas greeting is going to have to be short (ha-ha). Not because '99 hasn't been an eventful year for the Mendizza family, because it has. Boy! We did a bunch of stuff. Worked hard. Played hard. Sector Invested. Here are just a few things we did: got some new dishes (tell you about that a little later); had a flood (Lara forgot to turn the bath water off); climbed the ancient Mayan Pyramid at Chichen-Itza on the Yucatan peninsula and made a human sacrifice to gods in charge of the NASDAQ (you gotta try this!); Lara entered fifth grade; Sue and I became vegetarians; Lara became an object of desire (a guy named Dylan or Doolan fell in love with her); we read *The Hobbit* out loud; got a lead role in *Annie* (Lara); went to Paris, Andorra, Barcelona, Provence, Florence, Venice and Salzburg; became carnivorous, again; learned to sing "Camelot" real loud like Robert Goulet. And that was just April.

So, as usual, there's lots to say, and no one knows better than I how much you crave those long, elegant descriptions of detail, like the brand and pattern of china we selected, our new combination of antioxidants and of course the buzz about Lara and Doolie. That's why I've always written thirty- or forty-page Christmas letters like the one from last year that's still lying next to your toilet. But this year is difficult because of . . . well yes, because of Y2K.

In just a few weeks civilization is going to end—which is why we got our new china this year—and we feel our time would be better spent getting the used tires we need for the barricade we're building around our house trailer out in the Mojave. We laid the mines last weekend and we're moving out there with our weapons, our dehydrated gourmet meals and our Tony Bennett CDs around December 28. We obtained Department of Education authorized lesson modules for "Building a Family Militia" and "How to Drink Sand" and will home-school Lara in the desert until civilization gets back on its feet. Alas, even though it's Christmas and we love you a lot, when the end comes please don't try to call us or come out whining for food, because if you do we'll have to kill you. That's what the folks on the Internet tell us to do.

Since we have quite a few readers who are either in jail or fugitives from an unjust and onerous tax structure, we usually begin our Christmas greeting with a summary of all the exciting things that have happened this year in Southern California. We're going to skip that this year, though. The sun came up. Air temperature reached seventy-five degrees. Brad Pitt announced his engagement to another blond girl. And that was it. The sun went down on Southern California and (ha-ha) on Gwyneth Paltrow. We're resigned to the fact that Los Angeles has slipped off the screen as far as world-class media events are concerned. No more riots, fires, earthquakes. No killers set free, or not that many. Just a lot of peace and prosperity, like Brussels.

All you have to do is scan the entertainment pages to know that we've been scrubbed, media-wise. Here's a sample of the (ho-ho-ho) "stars" that are appearing in this season's big Hollywood films: Angus Macfadyen, Skeet Ulrich, Uma Somebody, Casper Van Dien, Saffron Burrows and Jewel. Somebody mind telling me what that is all about? Is anybody really going to care if Angus, Skeet and Uma bolt from rehab and have children out of wedlock with Casper, Saffron and Jewel? Naming stars after things we don't understand has greatly diminished our stature in the world media. Remember all the "Roberts" we used to have? Robert Stack, Robert Taylor, Robert DeNiro. Occasionally we'd even get a Rod or a William, but never a Skeet. These were stars with a capital S and good bankable consonant sounds. Compare them with Casper, Uma and Jewel. Our celebrities have clearly been trivialized, and thus we have been trivialized; for a society, as William Blake was so fond of saying, is only as good as the celebrities it has in rehab.

In an effort to protect our Lara from this kind of decline and to foster more authentic family values and hopefully even run across a few famous people with names that don't derive from trendy food menus, we decided to embark upon a quest, a family quest so to speak, to the ancient Mayan civilization that existed on the Yucatan peninsula in Mexico over a thousand years ago. Today this mystical enclave of deep esoteric knowledge and free markets is commonly known as Cancun. Our goal, of course, was to expose Lara to the rigors of a true spirit quest and to teach her something about how celebrities lived in earlier cultures.

Lara was very excited. She told us that she would love to go on a quest, especially if we took a limo to the airport and flew first class to the quest place. "No way," we said. Both Sue and I were adamant about this. It was going to be a character-building quest of the spirit, not one of those crass touristy trips with those gaudy stickers on all the luggage. Then I remembered that Ghandi had taken limos on his way to protest British colonial rule in India, and for sure the Dalai Lama drives around in Richard Gere's limo. So, we told Lara that the limo was OK (as long as you meditate and pray all the way to LAX), but that first class was out. "Oh Mommmmmmmm" she said. "No, sweetheart," Sue replied. "Being in coach is like fasting in the desert. It cleanses your soul." "That's right," I added in a sagacious tone. "Jesus and Britney Spears fasted in the desert and flew coach a lot before they became stars." Once we explained who Jesus was, Lara said OK, that she'd quest in coach, but insisted on ordering the McDonald's Kid's Meal for her fast.

Sue was excited about the trip, too. Spirit quests have always been a favorite thing of hers, and she spends a lot of her free time looking through the hundreds of catalogs that come in the mail—we must be on a quest list—with descriptions of quests to Maui, the quest to St. Croix and the famous six-spa quest that led to Cindy Crawford's spiritual breakthrough. So off we go. The limo pulled up in front of our house at 7:00 a.m. sharp, just as we requested. It was a long son-of-a-gun. The front of the vehicle was parked at our curb, while the rear was still, surprisingly, at LAX. We used cell phones inside the car to communicate with each other and it took us most of the trip time to figure out how to open the minibar and adjust the volume on the CD player. It was a fun, stress-free ride, though. And a smooth flight in coach to the Yucatan.

As we were landing, Lara could immediately tell she wasn't in the U.S. anymore. In fact she looked out the window during our descent and the first thing she said was, "This can't be the airport. Something must have gone wrong." The jungles of the Yucatan are very dense, but they don't look like the jungles in the movies. The growth is rather low to the ground, dense, flat and impenetrable, a little like swampland, which is what it used to be. "No, sweetheart," explains Sue. "This is it. The quest has begun."

"Can" in the ancient language of the Mayans means "long strip of land with huge cinderblock hotels crammed together like sardines on both sides of the street. "Cun" in Mayan means multitudes of sweaty tourists in tank tops." (Already we were teaching Lara the language.) We made our way to our hotel, the Hyatt Regency Caribe, where we were greeted by spirit guides who helped us check in and debit our American Express card. There were colorful peacocks strutting around the grounds like cocky dethroned aristocrats pining for lost and better times. We were offered big, succulent Mexican papayas and mangoes. Fronds of exotic palms swayed in the wind like women waving their hats. And when we opened the balcony doors inside our room and looked outside we gasped at the vista before us: there it was, the Caribbean! Or no, wait. "Is that the Caribbean or the Atlantic, honey?" I ask. "I think it's the Gulf of Mexico, sweetheart," says Sue. "No," says Lara. "I think it's the lagoon they created when they did the landfill, or maybe the Pacific." We're surrounded by water and it's very beautiful—aquamarine here, deep purple over there—but nobody knows which body of water is which, not even the natives, most of whom hail from Montebello.

Powerful winds were blowing from the east or west or south or whatever, causing a relentless and forbidding surf that pounded the coast and frothed up like the head on a schooner of beer (remember those quests?). The air of course was warm and full of moisture, and we gradually began to realize that we were in a tropical zone much different from our own culture and climate. So Lara and I quickly put on our shorts and our only tank tops and went downstairs to begin our adventure by playing a few games of what we called Typhoon Tennis.

It rained quite a bit on our first day. Of course, we were still recovering from coach and a little disoriented by the change in place and culture. So, in the afternoon, we did something really strange. We found ourselves running in the rain to catch one of the beat-up old buses that run tourists up and down the Cancun strip. We get off at the Kukulkan Mall (Kukulkan is one of the ancient Mayan gods and you'll find him everywhere on the Peninsula.). We walked into the mall and were startled by the glittering lights and pounding mall noise. "Hey," says Lara. "This is just like home." And except for all the ceramic Kukulkans, it was quite similar.

I know it sounds crazy for us to end up at the mall on the first day of our quest, but one has to "flow" on a quest and the currents, or maybe it was old Kukulkan himself, just seemed to coax us toward merchandise and the screening of "A Bug's Life" in Spanish. We ate dinner at an authentic Mayan restaurant called Ruth's Chris Steak House and for Sue it was a genuine breakthrough. "Oh my gosh," she says after finishing her steer, "I'm eating herd animals again. I used to eat like this all the time." See! The quest is working.

OK. Here's where one begins to wonder if one is wasting one's time reading about the family of one's—let's face it—rather distant acquaintance whom one doesn't really know or care for that much, and also about why one has to use this ridiculous word "one" when one actually means "you." Well, one can stop now if one wants to. But one will be in deep shit if one does. I mean I'm sure you have other things to do, like buying and consuming more stuff, but I must caution you: 100% of the people who completed reading last year's ludicrous Christmas letter advanced their net worth by 35% to 65% and/or had visions of an afterlife. Yet those who put the letter down, stuffed it in the drawer with the appliance warranties and take-out menus or left it behind the toilet without at least getting to the part about Lara's achievements in team sports suffered unexplainable setbacks in their personal and professional lives as well as losing their faith in God. It's your choice though. Lara's Mission Report is ahead (the one that all kids in California have to do in fourth grade), and you'll find out which brand and pattern of china we purchased. (Hint: Does V&B mean anything to you?) But first, our pilgrimage to the top of the pyramid at the sacred Mayan site of Chichen Itza. Wow. That was really strange.

Chichen Itza is a holy Mayan city about three hundred miles from the profane Mayan city of Cancun. You have to get up very early in the morning and take a bus to the ancient site, usually with a lot of people from Minneapolis. Our guide told us to meet him in the morning at a place called O'Brian's Tavern, which is apparently owned by a Mayan Shaman (medicine man) with knowledge of the ancient purification rites known cryptically as "Bloody Mary."

Sue and Lara wanted to sit in the back of the bus because we could all sit together. I whined about that for about half an hour, and then snuggled up against Lara on one side and a women from Pittsburgh with spiked blonde hair on the other. All during the ride I peered out the window and watched the monotonous jungle pass by like a vast interminable wall. Lara and Sue played that game where you name a city that starts with A, and then the next person has to name a city that starts with B and so on. By El Paso I was slipping into a kind of dreamy thought about the

Mayan people who lived here two thousand years ago.

Did they possess an advanced esoteric knowledge different from our modern understanding of things, as some people claim? And if they did, why didn't it result in the invention of a wheel or automatic weapons. I listened to the guide talk about the Mayan people, and as I did, gradually came to the realization that they probably did not possess a knowledge that was superior to our own. He told us that Mayans didn't rise and disappear mysteriously, as legend has it. They rose gradually. As their agriculture advanced, so did their powers of observation, because after all that's what happens when a culture discovers agriculture. They have to become better observers of the heavens and earth in order to plant crops on time, and to know when to harvest and what to have for Thanksgiving. Their ability to make empirical connections between the imaginings inside their heads (superstition) and the things that were actually taking place in the world around them (reality) improves. That's really what science is all about, comparing ideas with reality, and then making good bombs.

Regarding their decline, our guide said the Mayans simply lost their belief. The people began to lose their faith in their leaders and in their gods. They had some bad crops (maize) and life got tough. Then they began naming their movie stars after cartoon characters and that was really the nail in the coffin. In fact, recent translations of the hieroglyphics carved into their temple walls unveiled the first known use of the names "Uma" and "Spike." Soon after those names began showing up on pyramids, the society gradually dispersed and the civilization just fragmented into little villages, which still exist in the jungle today. By the time the Spaniards arrived, Chichen Itza was a ghost town.

Once one arrives at Chichen Itza and gets off the bus and

walks past the trees to the open plane upon which the great pyramid sits, however, all this skepticism fades away and one is struck by an eerie feeling of grandeur and awe. You bend your head way back and look up at the pyramid before you and you think Jesus! How did they do this 1,000 years ago? One can't help thinking that indeed something very special took place here and that maybe there is something to the idea of a unique, maybe even secret esoteric knowledge after all. We suddenly became reverent and our estimation of the Mayans went way up.

Lara was stunned, too, which is hard to achieve without a crystal display and million dollar Pixar graphics clutching her retina. The pyramid looms large in the big open square. It is monolithic, statuesque and serene. You can just imagine the square filling up with thousands of Mayans and the high priests standing on top of the awesome structure making pronouncements about how they, the priests, were able to get the sun to come up every day and the corn to grow and girls to like ugly guys. We wandered for hours through the abandoned temple ruins and really felt that the early people had chosen a very unique spot to raise their civilization. It felt a little like Sedona, Arizona, and Delphi in Greece, and maybe the new Bellagio Hotel in Las Vegas.

Lara and I coaxed and coaxed her, but Sue refused to make the climb to the top of the pyramid with us. She stood at the base, while Lara and I slowly, cautiously, negotiated the nine hundred and ninety nine steps (one for each year it took the Mayans to figure out which way was south) from the bottom to the top. There were no handrails, no safety devices, no attendants. You just climbed up all by yourself, which is in stark contrast to the way something like this might be handled in the U.S., where there would surely be a booth at the bottom in which the PI lawyers could line up like taxis waiting for fares. As we gradually ascended, Sue's figure below got smaller and smaller. The wind became cooler and fiercer and felt almost personal. Lara was nervous, especially as we got higher and higher, but she was also very courageous and determined, and I was right behind her. "Just one step at a time," I said to her. "And don't look down." Then I looked down. And then I said, much louder, "Jesus! Whatever you do, don't look down!"

The view from the top of the pyramid was majestic, a three-hundred-and-sixty degree panorama of the sacred site, the temple ruins, the observatory, and the jungle, which spread all the way to the horizon. Lara and I were up there together and it was so very, very unlike any other place I would normally be with her, like Von's. I was really a little anxious about our safety, because there was no safety up there. We were on our own. When we looked down, Sue was still there but no bigger than the period at the end of this sentence. We stood there together, the wind whispering secrets to us and our imaginations conjuring up weird thoughts, when suddenly the whole vista began to increase in brightness and as it did the people down below as well as the jungle, the air that surrounded us and everything else for as far as the eye could see began to shimmer slightly with an ever-increasing silvery intensity that was almost audible.

Whoa! I was a little stunned, but Lara was cool and steady. She had been reading a lot of books like The Chronicles of Narnia and Tolkein's Lord of the Rings series and knew this sort of thing happened occasionally. She took my hand and squeezed. The light became so bright that everything around us, including the pyramid beneath us, was gradually disappearing, so overcome were they by the intense illumination. Eventually they were just gone and we were for a moment standing together in what seemed like midair—though it was more like midspectre—with nothing but the Mayan wind and Lara's faith to console us.

"Just breathe, Dad," Lara said, recalling similar adventures she had seen on the Disney Channel. I breathed. Next, a wall rose out of nowhere and began to create an enclosure around us, still very bright, still shimmering, but outlines of a pathway toward we knew not what began to appear. Together, we walked straight ahead, and eventually came upon a gigantic . . . what: altar? Tabernacle? "This is a Disney thing, isn't it?" I said to Lara. "No way," she responded. "Disney would have theme music and novelty items."

We approached the golden façade of the altar and in the intense white light we began to make out the shadowed outline of an inscription on the stone. "I don't have my glasses, sweetheart. What's it say?" I asked. "Dad," she responded. "You don't wear glasses. And it doesn't say anything. It's like a picture or symbol of something. Looks like an icon." Lara pressed down on the icon and the face of the golden tabernacle opened and across the vast blank plane appeared six mathematical calculations. "Hey. Just like our extra credit math sheets at school," said Lara with the delight of recognizing something familiar in an utterly strange and foreign experience. "Do you know what they mean?" I asked, thinking the mushrooms I had with my steak at Ruth's Chris Steak House must have been the cause of this whole thing. "They don't mean anything," she says. "You just solve them." "Well, solve them, honey! Can't you see we're in the middle of a hallucination here?"

Lara studied the mathematical expressions and one by one, solved them inside her head. As she determined the answer, she uttered the solution out loud. With each utterance, the formula vanished and a letter, not a Mayan hieroglyph, but a nice modern Greco-Roman letter appeared where the formula had existed.

"It's a code! Dad. It's like we do at school. We solve the equation and it gives a letter. Get all the letters and it spells a word. Get the word and you get extra points." "Get the points, and you go to Stanford, right?" I said. "Daaaaad! You get a star and a Tootsie Roll," she responded.

The first letter was Q. The second was A. Eventually there were six letters: QADSAN. But it meant nothing to me and nothing to Lara either. "It must be a Mayan word for something," I say, "an ancient evocation of a deep spiritual force for transforming the soul." "No," she replies. "I think it's just backwards. They always try to trick you like that." "Really?" I say. Lara spelled out the letters in reverse: NASDAQ. My eyes opened wide. A brilliant transparent flash blinded us and all I can say before everything went blank was "NASDAQ! Of course."

The next thing I know, Sue, Lara and I are lying around together on the big king-sized bed at the Hyatt Regent Caribe listening to the Caribbean Sea, the Atlantic Ocean and the Gulf of Mexico pummel the shore with their windblown waves. Sue is eating three chicken curries and what room service calls a "family flan." Lara is eating a hamburger. And I am lying on my back holding a *Betty and Veronica* comic book up in the air, reading out loud to the girls about the ways in which Betty and Veronica vie for Archie's infantile affections (something they've been doing for at least fifty years to no avail and without even graduating from high school). Duh!

Lounging around on the big bed, eating room service and reading Archie comics was probably as meaningful and precious to us, and maybe at an even deeper level, than the magic moments on top of the ancient pyramids. And in spite of her dad's cognitive issues and the superficial qualities of Cancun itself, Lara really did learn a few things about Mexico. Language. Flag. Currency.

Cuisine. The important thing was not to teach her what we all think of as authentic culture, but to just show her that there are places in the world that are really quite different from Trabuco Canyon. Appreciation of authentic culture will mature as Lara matures. I asked her what she had learned and she said, "They have a lot of people doing one job. Like instead of one person getting a taxi for you, there are three people getting the taxi. One blows the whistle. One opens the door. And one tells the taxi driver where to go." "Good, Good. What else?" "Sometimes they bargain for things instead of just paying the price. They go, 'Oh my friend, that's way too low.'"

I tried to teach Lara how to bargain, but she just kept laughing at me. I whispered to her in a secretive, conspiratorial tone: "When they say the hand painted Kulkulcaan plates are twenty dollars, I want you to hold your stomach and pretend to cry. Say something about not having eaten any food since Cinco de Mayo, OK? They'll drop the price to fifteen dollars if you do that." And she just laughed. She'd say, the people in Mexico don't have as much money as we do. How come? And I'd say, that's a long story.

On our last day, Sue and Lara and I are sitting at a table on the patio waiting for lunch to be served. I am dazed as usual. I just sit there, letting all the big questions about life and destiny pass by, just sit there and stare out at the turquoise-colored sea and watch the migration of clouds and the fine, unequivocal line of the horizon. The sound of the surf is still powerful and relentless. Sue is sitting across the table from me, and to my disbelief I see that she is beginning to make plans for the next trip, the one to Europe. Holy shit! She starts articulating the things that must be done, and diagramming various options on a mind map. "I don't want to plan our next trip right now," I say. "I just want to sit here and look at the clouds and savor the last few moments of this trip. What are you doing?" She gently explains to me why she is looking ahead. She says, "If I don't start planning our next trip, I will be so heartbroken about this one ending that I won't be able to stand it. It's the only way I know to keep from being sad." I think to myself, what an extraordinary person Sue is. On our way back, we lighten up and give each other new names: "Wrinkle, Twinkle and Hot Tamale." I'll let you guess who is whom.

Ok, here's the bragging part. Christmas letters are traditionally used to express the innate superiority of the author's kids over the reader's. It's a subtle, but unmistakable art form, which documents our children's progress on their journey from being carefree, spirited and super imaginative individuals toward the ultimate goal of becoming boorish, inhibited, brain-dead adults, commonly referred to as "good citizens." Our Lara, of course is like, way superior, at least as far as Sue and I are concerned. She is the youngest in a class of GATE (Great-at-Everything) kids. She's a straight A student, which means she has mastered the great art of filling out worksheets. She has become very competitive on the tennis court, too. She's winning matches and gets better every week it seems. "I beat all the boys, today," she says, which she totally loves to do. And more importantly she's still having fun, especially with her first team-tennis tournament.

One of the hardest things for a parent to do I think is to try to rise above the winning and losing syndrome in these sporting events. You tell yourself over and over that it doesn't matter. They should just be having fun. Improving their skills. Standings don't matter, at all. And then there's real life. Lara is playing a girl two years older and twice her size and its five games to five in a first-to-win-six match. Deep inside I'm going, "It doesn't matter. It doesn't matter. It doesn't matter." I try to think of what the Dalai Lama would do. I recite old mantras that I learned from Baba Ram Dass in the seventies. I hope she wins, of course, but it doesn't matter, it doesn't matter, it doesn't matter. But if it doesn't matter, why has my heart stopped? And why are the paramedics phoning in Sue's vital signs to ER?

While it's natural to highlight their outward achievements in sports and academics, it seems a shame that we don't boast equally about how kind our kids have become, or how sensitive, or intuitive. The reasons are obvious. It's national security: if we're going to kick ass on the new European Union and keep the People's Republic of China in its place, we need math wizards and entrepreneurs, not empathy and kindness. The national curriculum from kindergarten to graduate school is recalibrated each year to meet those ultimate objectives. Nevertheless, it was not a tangible skill, but an advancement in sensibility and emotional texture that struck me this year as the most significant milestone of Lara's childhood journey. It was the way in which she responded to her gradual awareness that a boy named Dylan (fictitious name) liked her.

At first, she couldn't believe it, couldn't fathom it or find a familiar place for it inside of herself. But there it was; Dylan likes me. I might be a little biased, but to me Lara's reaction has been unique; unique I mean for a nine-year-old. What I mean is, she wasn't giddy. She was thoughtful. Astounded in a way. Filled with a genuine wonder at the fact that it was actually happening. I thought it rather wondrous and mysterious, too: the way in which we "enter" one another's lives.

I found out about it in the car after I picked the girls up from school on a Thursday. Lara and Kristina and Jessica were in the back seat. I said, "Did Deena do anything funny at school, today?" Lara said, "Yeah, she did. She made her apple sauce." "What do you mean?" "She puts her apple in a plastic bag and then smashes it on the table. Voila! Applesauce." And then Lara just casually said that a boy in her social studies class has a crush on her.

The world suddenly skidded to a stop! Everyone's interest was piqued. I tried to be cool, though, and decided not to go out and buy a handgun right away. I asked, "How do you know?" And Lara says matter-of-factly, "Because he acts very odd whenever I am around. The other boys in the class told me that when I'm not there he behaves one way, and when I'm there he behaves quite differently. He starts playing around, showing off and stuff." "Maybe he's just trying to get your attention," I say. And she says, "Yes, I think he's just trying to get my attention." That's it. I'm buying the gun.

At dinner I encourage Lara to talk about it, still holding back on my male instinct to disembowel the perpetrator of this foul and lascivious act. As we sipped the minestrone soup that Sue had prepared, I made a few delicate inquiries.

"It's just soooo weird," Lara recalls. "Dylan and I walked all the way from social studies class to the bike racks together. I mean we were walking side by side!" Ahhhh Haaaaa! I knew it. The old bike rack routine! "What were you doing?" I asked, calmly. "Just having a conversation," she said. "He told me about the different voices he could impersonate. And I said like Robin Williams, because you know how Robin Williams can do all those different voices? And then we started talking about Robin Williams. And oh my god, it was so . . ." And she paused, unable really to describe how strange the experience was. "I don't know. It was just so unusual."

We continued to talk about her experience with Dylan for a long time. The conversation went from one thing to another. She told me about how Dylan can make a sound like an elephant. And I'm thinking yeah, yeah, yeah. I used to make animal sounds myself. She told us how she has noticed him raising his head from his book when she enters the room, raises his head to look at her and then puts it back down and then moments later raises it back up again. And I think: A definite sign of sinister intent! She tells us how he always starts joking around when she comes and sits down next to him. "I didn't even know who Dylan O'Donnel was. I didn't even know he existed. Then we had our seat assignments changed and there he was." And then she raised her arms up into the air and said with great emotion, "Isn't it just incredible, how one small little tiny event can just all of a sudden change your whole life?" And I really did calm down, and thought to myself, yes it is, sweetheart. Pretty damned incredible.

Then Lara adds, in this surprisingly thoughtful way, "The strange part of this whole thing is that you just don't know what is going to happen next. When I go back to school tomorrow will he still like me? Will it go on, you know, to the next thing?" And I think, if Dylan is dead it won't. But I don't say that. I stay calm and attain to an adult perspective. Then my heart rises up into my throat. It's just so precious: the careful, perceptive, sensitive way she is handling this new experience.

After our conversation at the dinner table, I pick Lara up in my arms and hold her and she kisses me. And then she says, "It's not like you, Daddy. I mean I know you." And I say, "Yeah, And I can't make that elephant noise." And she says, "Yeah." And I say, a little defensively, "But I can talk like Donald Duck!"

A couple of weeks later I came home after getting final artwork off to a magazine and Lara was there at the door to greet me. Sue, who has been ill with the stomach flu all day, is sitting on the white sofa, of all places (we never sit on the white sofa), and she says to me: "Lara is Molly!" I furrow my forehead, which seems to be increasing significantly in overall surface area, and I go, "Huh?" Lara is Molly? And then I get it. "Are you serious? Lara is Molly! Molly! You're kidding. You're not kidding. Whoa! That is wonderful! You did it, honey. You got the part!" Lara had been auditioning for a principal role in her school production of Annie and she got it. I know it doesn't matter, but it feels so good. We high five. I give her a big hug. Then I say, we've got to go practice baseball. You have your first practice tomorrow and I want to see if you remember how to bat and catch.

So we played some baseball this year. It's the first year Lara played a team sport. We held back on team sports because the fields were so crowded with adults that there really wasn't room for another kid to play. You've got two or three umpires, a head coach, an assistant coach, a manager, a chaperone, a snack-person, two base-running coaches, a scorekeeper, a photographer, a groundskeeper, a league representative, a ball-parent, a team counselor, the guy to measure the distance from the pitcher's mound to the plate to within Plank's constant and of course a couple of lawyers to arbitrate disputes. Plus some volunteer parents to just stand around and be ready to say "Way to go" whenever a kid does something good.

Team sports for kids are really an activity for AWLs: Adults Without Lives. Platoons of them stand around telling the girls what to do, and the girls just try to do everything they're asked. The kids very rarely say anything or know what the score of a game is. But they love being together, playing around and helping their parents feel good about themselves. Most of the really fun stuff takes place off the field, in the dugout, driving to and from the game, and then afterward when they get their Ding Dongs. I hated the thought of Lara getting caught up in the sports miasma of AWLs, but she really wanted to play, and not only did she learn a lot and improve her play, but most of my apprehensions did not find ground in reality. The managers and coaches were very kind people, with just a slightly perverse bias for winners. And the girls did toughen up. You could tell by the chants one heard coming from the dugout. "We don't play with Barbie Dolls. We just play with bats and balls. Sound off. Onetwo."

We played baseball. We sang in Annie. We beat the boys at tennis. We got our leg in the right place during our glissade jete and glissade ensemble (ballet movements). We became vegetarians. In fact every kid at school became a vegetarian at one point or another. Not because they didn't like hamburgers anymore, but because it just sounded so cool at the lunch table to say, "I don't eat meat." It goes like, "Do you want my sandwich?" And then they get to say, "No thanks. I don't eat meat." And everybody goes wow! You don't eat meat. How cool. When Lara came home and said it at dinner I responded with my usual well-thought-out inquiry, "If God didn't want us to eat animals, why did he make them out of meat?" And Lara said, "Daaaaaaaaaaaaad!"

So, it was love, baseball, Annie, ballet, tennis. It was a "Mission Report." And a "County" report. Fifty reports on Native American peoples, and the contributions they have made to our current civilization, like blue corn. It was 304,567 work sheets. Time passed. Love faded. And by the beginning of fifth grade Dylan is, as they say, history. In fact nobody can find Dylan. He just disappeared. His face is on milk cartons, now, and he looks pretty good there, but nobody can point the finger at me because I have an air-tight alibi. I was in Europe helping Lance Armstrong win the Tour de France.

You've probably noticed that I haven't said too much about what Sue and I have done this year, that most of the narrative has focused on Lara. There's a good reason for that, of course: Christmas letters are supposed to tell folks about the kids. But I know you're curious, so here's what Sue and I have done this year: Work, sleep and nag. That's it. We work. We sleep. And we nag. Work. Sleep. Nag. Work. Sleep. Nag Work. Sleep. Nag Work. Sleep. Nag Work. Sleep. Nag Work. Sleep. Nag Work. Sleep. Nag Work. Sleep. Nag Work. Sleep. Nag Work. Sleep. Nag Work. Sleep. Nag Work. Sleep. Nag.

True, I published a couple of poems. Sue took up the study of Feng Shui, graduated her one-hundredth felon at the jail college and got a new device to make her face look like Suzanne Somers'. But that was about it. Other than that we worked, slept and nagged Lara.

As you know, nagging is an ancient and highly respected parental art, with many techniques and exotic styles. One that I really like is the "universal double nag." You do a single nag and before any kid could possibly complete the task you follow up with a quick sharp secondary nag. "Do your spelling; did you do your spelling? Read your book. Have you read your book? Take a sweater. —Did you take your sweater? Brush your teeth; did you brush your teeth?" Then you have your stupid-question nag. "Aren't you cold? Aren't you hot? Are you going to eat that broccoli?" Sometimes I even like to use the pretentious foreign language nag like, "Practice your glissade jete? S'il vous plait." But the real workhorse, the nag you can always rely upon when you don't feel too creative, is the basic hygiene nag. You just give it a simple, "Wash your hair. Brush your teeth. Clean up your room. Take your bath. Pick up your clothes." After about your fifth year as a parent you'll find yourself using some spectacular nag combinations and even inventing some unique nags of your own, like the "chain nag" where you string a whole bunch of nags together as a nice way to end the day. "Do your homework. Don't jump on the furniture. Go to bed. Hey! Why aren't you in bed? Turn off the light." Followed by the morning refrain nag of, "Get up. Jesus! Aren't you up yet?"

Here's an example of what I call a mega-nag. I was on the floor with all of Lara's schoolwork spread out before me, trying to make a list of the things she had to complete. "Did you finish Maniac Magee?" "Yes." "Then finish the packet. It's not hard. Just some reading comp." "We don't have to finish the whole packet." "How much do you have to finish?" "We just need to finish the chapters that I've read." "But you've read all the chapters, haven't you? I mean you said you finished the book." "I said I've read way ahead. That doesn't mean I finished." "Wait a minute. You mean you haven't finished the whole book?" "I didn't say I haven't finished. I said I didn't necessarily finish." We went on and on and I could not figure out, or get a clear answer from Lara about how much of the work sheet she was supposed to complete.

So I get frustrated, and at that moment Sue walks by and criticizes me for something I did way back when I was about four years old. I go "Huh?" Like, excuse me for being born. I can tell she is angry with me for pressing Lara on the homework. (Note: Parenting is always and forever a "Good Cop/Bad Cop" endeavor.)

And so I do the appropriate thing, and throw a tantrum. I wad up the homework and say, "That's it. I'm out of here. You guys do the homework yourselves." I go upstairs and sit down at my desk and furiously pretend to do something that's very important to the future of the nation, like disposing of all the old "post-its" that look like a yellow windblown wreath around the computer monitor. Later, Lara comes in. She and Sue are going somewhere. From the doorway she says, in her sweet, forgiving, purely benevolent voice, "Bye, Daddy." I feel like Dr. Mengele. I say, "Bye-bye, sweetheart. But I still think you should get the daily math sheets from Mrs. Brown." She pauses and says, "Goodbye, anyway." (Like even though you're still angry, I'm going to be the bigger person and say, "Goodbye, anyway." And she is, in a lot of ways, much bigger.)

"Welcome to Orly Airport," says the cabin attendant as we taxi toward the terminal. "The time is approximately 11:00." It had been a very long journey from curbside Trabuco Canyon, across the North Atlantic to the continent, and we were so tired that everything seemed a little unreal. "I feel like I am in a movie," Lara says. "Yeah," I reply. "Our bodies are here, but our minds are still in Orange County." Then I turn to the French woman sitting next to me during the flight and say, "What do they mean approximately 11:00? These are the pilots. Don't they know exactly what the time is here?" She grins and says, "You're in Paris, now, monsieur."

Like purchasing our new china settings, we felt that anything dependent on civilization should really be done in 1999. We wanted Lara to see what the European continent looked like before Western technology destroys it and we have to launch our new life as a family militia in the Mojave. We began in Paris, of course, because that is where civilization reached its pinnacle. "The French have created more ways to make a ham sandwich than any other people," I explain to Lara. She blinks. "And that is the earmark of a truly advanced culture." She blinks again and says, "What about the shopping?" And her mother and I just beam as we make our descent into Orly, so proud are we of the values and rich historical sense we have already instilled in our daughter.

The taxi driver who drove us from Orly to our hotel in the St. Germane de Pres area of the city was very flamboyant. Parlez vous Ingles? No. No, he says. Je parle Francais and a little espanol. Oh good. Sue can speak with him in Spanish, and she tries. But his Spanish and her Spanish never really connect. He yelled at the traffic for us, and pretended that he didn't quite know where the hotel was located, banging his finger on the map and shrugging his shoulders so hard he got big wobbly jowls. Then he flailed his arms and screamed in French at all the tiny Renaults and Peugeots that cut in front of him. He's up for a Tony this year for best all-around performance as a French taxi driver, and made a very good impression on Lara, who actually applauded.

"Look," I say to Lara as we skirt through Paris traffic. She looks. "Look at how small the cars are." She goes, yeah, they look like cars in Disneyland. I feel a lesson coming. Why do you think they are so small? Why aren't there any SUVs? "Because we're a lot fatter than the French people?" she guesses. "Good guess, but no. It's because gasoline costs so much here. It's also because the cars had to be made small enough to get down the narrow medieval avenues, but mostly because Europeans tax their gasoline so much that it's twice the price as in the U.S." And Lara asks, "What do they do with the money?" "Give everybody health insurance," I say.

The room at the Lindbergh Hotel is not ready yet, and so, tired and hallucinating from jet lag, we take our first walk in the City of Lights. It's midday though, and the only light is coming from an arc weld sun in a pewter-colored sky. It's hot, and the air is approaching the temperature of the human body. In fact, that's what the boulevard feels like in this dreamy state that we are in, like a body, a hot, moist body with a pulse and mind and stream of consciousness. We negotiate the crowds and traffic. The windows of the storefronts glare in the sun and there are big signs everywhere that say, SOLDE. Eventually we find ourselves close to the oldest church in Paris. It's called Saint-Germain-des-Pres. We walk the busy boulevard toward the worn steeple that rises above the skyline, but before we actually reach the church, we come to a crossroad. To the right we see something that looks like a street carnival: hundreds of yellow balloons, crowds forming and a pounding, European rock music from speakers the size of refrigerators.

"Quick," I say. "It's Euro-Trash! Run! Get to the church." And it's open, thank God. We go in. It's dark. Quiet. The stones are old and cool. It feels as if we have entered a magnificent natural cavern like one might discover in the mountains of New Mexico. It's medieval, though. The oldest structure Lara has ever entered. We savor the respite from the glare and edgy heat outside. Sue and I and Lara walk around the old church, looking up at the vaulted ribs that are the universal infrastructure for most old churches. It does seem vast and holy and mysterious. Dark alcoves that are barred by iron gating to prevent people from going into them contain statues of saints. Lara doesn't know what a saint is, as yet. And I'm trying to think of a way to explain it. How does one explain saint? "They're like angels before they become angels. They're like friends of God, who help us understand the divine. They're just real good people who do miracles, like Zena."

We make another turn and come upon a group of young

people who are sitting before an alcove that houses a beautiful image of the Virgin. They begin to sing, a capella. Their voices rise up and fill the cathedral with a redemptive polyphonic sound that is chant and song and prayer all mixed together. It is lovely. I lift Lara onto my lap and we listen, so thankful for the peace and rest.

But then, from outside the church, that pounding sound of Euro-rock begins to pummel the walls of the church and assault our threadbare sensibilities, as if the sanctuary were under siege by a hundred-thousand watts of secular electronic battering ram. Inside, the human voices coalesce in a soft, healing testament of faith and beauty. The outside blare of bad, sweaty, rock "n"roll music shreds the fabric of serenity inside. We are told by someone that the carnival forming outside is the first day of a gay pride celebration, humans reveling in their right to be and do whoever and whatever they want. I hold Lara close and think to myself, this is the world: so beautiful and raw.

We leave the oldest church in Paris a little confused and make our way back toward the hotel. Inside our minds it's about three o'clock in the morning. But here in Paris it's about noon, and everyone is having their lunch in the little cafes and brasseries that line the streets; actually the cafes are in the middle of the street and the cars just swerve around us. We find a table, and sit, stare like the dumb tourists we are at the menu. The French couple next to us is very kind. They slide their chairs over so the three of us can fit in. They tell us that it's Saturday, and there's a big sale on and everyone in Paris is taking advantage of it. That's why we see the word "SOLDE" on every window. It means "Sale."

They ask if they might help us with the menu. "I think we've got it," says Sue, who is fluent in German and Spanish and feels like there should be some transference of vocabulary into

French. Sue orders tortes. When the waitress brings us a big wedding cake made out of ham and cheese, we say maybe we could use a few pointers. Torte in Spanish means sandwich. In French it means pastry. In English of course, it means you're getting sued. The little cars are buzzing past the sidewalk café and Lara, ever alert to novelty, says, "Look, it's just like Diane said. They really do park their cars on the sidewalk in Paris."

We took a nighttime tour of the city and that was really an inspired thing to do, because to me that's when Paris is the most beautiful and the most like its old reputation as the City of Lights. The automobile, unfortunately, has decimated much of the charm that I'm sure used to fill the air here during the daytime. But at night the city shimmers, and almost outruns one's imagination.

During our visit, Paris was preparing itself for Bastille Day which celebrates the beginning of the French Revolution. The peasants, people like me and you, rose up against an aristocracy that had abused for centuries privileges that they had not earned. And so, we killed them. Who can forget that famous moment when an aide came running into Marie Antoinette's boudoir and told her that the people had no ham and cheese sandwiches to eat, and she replied with utter disdain, "Let them eat torte."

As we crossed the Seine for the first time, we saw a gigantic Ferris wheel sparkling against the darkening sky, and of course that's the historical site Lara wanted to see. What about Napoleon, I ask? "He's waited this long," she replies. "He can wait 'til we ride the Ferris wheel." And suddenly, I feel another lesson coming on. "There are two parts to Paris," I say to Lara. "The Left Bank, where all the creative people live, the poets and writers and people with really good hair. And then there's the Right Bank where all the rich people live." Lara thinks and then says,

"I like the right bank." And I say, "Yeah, you are a Right Bank kind of person."

We spent a few days in Paris, doing as many of the obligatory things as we could fit in, the pilgrimage to the Impressionist painters, up the Eiffel Tower, the glimpse of the Mona Lisa, and the experiencing indignant complaints about how rude the French people are to Americans (even though they were delightful to us). But the moments that were special to Sue and me were the one's outside the scope of guide books. Running in the rain through the Tuileries with Lara. Carrying her on my shoulders as we walked along the Seine, pretending to lose my balance and threatening to spill us both into the river. Sitting in the café as a family trying to figure out together how much to pay for a cup of coffee. "It says here, Comptour / d/f coffes crème is 15 francs, and the Salle / d/f coffee crème is 28 francs. Do you understand any of that, honey?" I ask. "No one does," Sue responds. "And they change it every day to keep us confused." She advises me to just wad up all the francs I have in my hand and hold it out to the waiter and hope that he remembers all the nice things we did for them during World War II.

We did learn one important thing in France, though. The French don't really eat snails. That is just a joke they play on Americans who feel so culturally inferior. French chefs created the rumor that eating snails was very sophisticated. They knew that Americans would eat anything they thought was genuinely French. So, they serve us snails. And as we eat them, the whole staff of the restaurant peers through a little window and watches in hysterical laughter. Next to voting against the U.S. in the United Nations, watching Americans eat snails is their most jovial form of entertainment.

OK. I know. It's getting late. Y2K is almost here and we're not even to Barcelona yet. So, we'll take the express train from here on. Actually it was the night train we took. Ten hours on a night train from Paris to the top of the Pyrenees Mountains and the little hamlet known as Andorra. It's a small sovereign nation nestled in the mountains between France and Spain, populated by lots of intriguing people with family crests and most of the money that used to be in Russia.

There were six of us in one sleeping compartment; Lara and Sue were on the two bottom bunks. I was in the middle bunk, and across from me was Phil, a recent college graduate making his frugal backpack tour across Europe before going back home and starting some IPOs and retiring at an age when I was still trying to decide whether or not to change my name to "Loving Light." (Don't you just hate this new generation of billionaires?) To sort of balance things out on the top bunks were two giggling girls from Norway. One could tell they were talking about sex by the way they giggled, but one could not guess exactly what they were saying, which makes the two girls' behavior quite similar to men at important sales meetings.

It was a wonderful lesson in communal living for Lara and a rather grueling ten-hour sleepless ordeal for moi. While chatting with Phil about what he was going to do with his first zillion dollars, I rolled over and felt Lara pulling at my fingers from the bunk below. Feeling her little hand there in the dark opened the moment for me. What a family experience: Sue and Lara and I trundling along in the dark train, all across the French countryside, gradually becoming more accustomed to the strange environment, the claustrophobia slowly opening up inside to a comfortable resignation; and the dull constant drone of the big train moving over track settling into a kind of dark lullaby which put everyone but me into a deep sleep. It was an "experience" that I hoped would find a place inside of Lara, one upon which she could build and expand. Because that is what this vacation was all about for me, not the sites, but seeing things together, being together in moments that are not momentous, not recorded, barely even perceived so deep and silent do they run within us. But someday, it is our hope that she may even be able to have sex in Norwegian.

After what seemed like a month of night, the morning light began to break. It was raining in the mountains. When the train stopped, a startling silence fell over us, like when the leaf-blowers in your neighborhood stop howling. It was wet and cold and fresh, but we were pretty dazed, and barely able to throw our sixteen pieces of luggage off the train before it set out again for Barcelona. Strangely, the train depot in Andorra isn't even close to Andorra. It was more like a deserted wooden hut thirty miles away. There was nothing for miles around and we felt like refugees in a cold and foreign land, with only about a $30,000 credit limit to get us through. We stood there in the cold, looking at each other and counting our Hartmans, thinking: does Fernando really exist, or was he just someone we dreamed? Suddenly, way down at the other end of the tracks, emerging from an ethereal mist like the ones in all the black and white movies from the 1940s, we see two small figures sharing a large umbrella and walking toward us. They gradually come into focus, and it's them. Fernando and Sonia have come to pick us up and show us Andorra and Spain. "Ole!"

Our stay with the famous Bontempi family—they have one of those crests, and a good share of rubles—meant more to us than I can really say: friendship in a foreign land, kids for Lara to play with (Luka and Karla), insights into culture and Russian money laundering. But as much as the love and kindness meant to us it was nothing compared to the greatest gift of all, which of course was free food. Do you have any idea what it costs to feed a family of three on the road in Europe? If you're ever planning a trip to Spain, you have to call us up first and get Fernando's phone number. He'll feed you for free, and once you get into the house and take over a bedroom, it is very hard for Spanish people to kick you out.

We had picnics in the Pyrenees, where Lara and Karla and Luka climbed the big boulders and waded in the running waters of early summer. From a little bridge over the stream, Fernando holds his daughter Karla by her feet and dips her head into the cold waters. Karla screams with laughter and shock. Fernando says it's an old Catalonian custom, and I grab Lara and say its time you were anointed, Catalonian style. Her head drops down to the water, and she splashes the little rapids with her hands. She's so happy. Later, Fernando and I sit and look at the way in which the wild flowers arrange themselves along the bank. "People spend years trying to copy that," he says.

After a few days in Andorra, Fernando and Sonia drove us to Barcelona where we experienced the robust Catalonian love of life and a generosity so bold and true that one can only imagine such a thing happening in Lara's story books. I'd never been to Spain before. Now that I have, I understand why its culture has become so ubiquitous and admired (other than the fact that Cortez and the guys conquered everybody they bumped into, and then asked them all nicely to speak Spanish and play the guitar).

Next, we went to the Costa Brava on the Mediterranean coast, a little-known retreat called Ampurias, where medieval ruins were atop Roman ruins which were atop Greek ruins. We swam in the sea and occasionally I would lecture. "Africa is right over there," I'd say to Lara, pointing across the blue water, and at the same time catching a glimpse of the bare-breasted women that were wading out waist-deep. "And France is over . . . err . . . no I mean over there." "Yeah," Lara would respond, "and the ice cream cart is right over there. Let's go."

While driving us to the train station to pick up our connection to Southern France, Fernando told us that the width of the train track in Spain was a little narrower than the train track in the rest of Europe. "It was a way to discourage invasion," he said, and it struck me as one of those little pieces of trivia that could extrapolate to explain the entire history of the European continent. Walls. Fortresses. Tricky train tracks. It didn't prevent us from invading the Bontempis though, and we're a little concerned that perhaps we overstayed out welcome. Fernando dropped us off at the train station and we tearfully said our farewells, and then we think he went back to Barcelona and Andorra and changed all his phone numbers. We haven't, alas, heard from him since.

We went to Provence for three reasons, to find Cézanne, cheer on Lance Armstrong during the Tour de France and eat snails. When we arrived, they told us that Cézanne was dead, which was a big disappointment. We were very pleased, though when we heard that Lance was winning stage races and acquiring a pretty good lead overall. When he whizzed by us, Lara held up a big sign that said, "Go Lance" and I, pretending like I was fifteen years younger than I really am (chronologically, that is) yelled, "Go dude!" and "We love you, man!" Sue was looking at a snail menu and pretending that I was a mentally handicapped relative that fate had placed in her custodial care. Anyway, it worked. Lance won. No one gave us much credit, but we weren't looking for that. After all, it's like the great philosopher Arthur Schopenhauer said, "It's just amazing how much you can accomplish if you don't have to worry about who gets the credit."

After getting our fill of snails and enjoying the hysterical laughter from French kitchens all over Provence, we packed up and drove to Florence (Firenze), Italy. It was a beautiful, curving drive through hundreds of tunnels all along the Cote d'Azur, past Nice and Monaco and other places where Monarchs hide out from angry peasants. As soon as you cross the border from France into Italy, a sudden change takes place. Everyone starts waving their hands as they talk and in their hands, there is always a prosciutto and melon sandwich, which was a unique twist on the French ham and cheese. We were going to Florence to see the Renaissance, of course, but when we arrived we were told that it wasn't there any more, that it went on tour about 500 years ago and never returned. So, we showed Lara all the cathedrals they left behind and peeked at Michelangelo's David and then we spent the rest of our trip inside the jewelry shops buying Florentine gold amulets and stuff. The price of gold hasn't been this low in decades and when Y2K hits, gold should go sky high. So it was really an investment.

Loaded with gold, we drove to the most charismatic city in the world, Venice. It was a long hard drive and we only had one night, but we thought Lara should see this place. You can't drive into Venice, of course, which is one of the things that make it so unique. So, we parked our car and left all our clothes and stuff locked in the trunk. Then, with just one change of underwear in a little backpack, we walked to a ferry, which would take us across the lagoon.

My god. It is such a unique place. What was it that Fernando said about civilization? People just kept trying things. And it's true. One day, over a thousand years ago, some guys sitting around a table bullshitting and pretending to do important work so they wouldn't have to help their wives at home, came up with this idea, "Hey! I know. Let's build a city on top of the water." "Not a bad idea," says another guy. "Nobody will be able to attack us and it will take us centuries to build." "Right, so we won't have to help in the kitchen for three hundred years." "Done," says the Doge. And today we have Venice.

We lug our bags over one canal bridge after another and finally reach San Marcos Square. A spectral fantasy. An ephemeral vision. An incomparable emanation of art and commerce. How did they do this? Even Lara is awestruck.

We locate our hotel, and it's a gem. We wash our faces. We go back down, and I walk up to the desk clerk and ask, "Are there any concerts tonight?" Venice of course is renown for a lot of things, but classical music is one of the renownest, and during the summer there should be some really great performances. He says one of the best chamber orchestras in Venice is playing tonight. YES! Our one night in Venice and we get to see the best. I ask him if I can go in my shorts. He frowns, shakes his head and says it wouldn't be a good idea. Shoot. Here we are in Venice, the city of Vivaldi and Corelli and a bunch of other "elli's" and I don't have any long pants.

I ask the clerk if I can buy some long pants, "Cheapeo," I emphasize. He writes the name of the Venetian equivalent of Wal-Mart on a piece of paper. We have an hour before the concert begins. Sue and Lara go get a bite to eat, and I race off through the dark, ancient, circuitous alleys of Venice in search of a pair of long pants.

Staggering through the city of Titian, Vivaldi, Marco Polo and Casanova, I beseech every Italian waiter and shopkeeper I come across with my urgent plea for directions. I point at the little paper and say: "Cheapio Storeo! Cheapeo Mallio, Grazi Grazi. I need a pair of cheap pantinettos, Ok? Grazi." There must have been a lot of guys like me running down the alleyways, because every time I tossed out the word, "cheapeo" the waiter or the shop keeper would point me in the right direction.

Finally, I locate the store. I race up to the men's section and furiously look through the pants for my size. When I pull up the tag and look, however, I despair. Size 162; Waist 17A; Length 106C. Jesus! What have they done? Listed all these pants in Italian sizes, for God's sake. So, I just grab a bunch of them and start trying them on. The sales lady politely walks up to me and asks me to do my changing in the dressing room, which I cordially do. I find a pair that fit OK in the waist, but they're way, way too long. So, I run out onto the floor and find a blue shirt. I take it into the dressing room, take out all the pins and put on the shirt. Then I use the pins to tack up the cuffs of the pants. TaaaaDaaa! I'm dressed. I pay for the clothes and run back to meet Sue and Lara who have just finished their prosciutto and melon pizza. We have a couple of minutes left.

Now all we have to do is find the church where the concert is to be performed. Down the ancient alleys once again. But instead of calling out the word cheapeo. I'm now pleading for directions to Chiesea San Bartolomeo. "Bartolomeo?" I say about every hundred yards. "Bartolomeo!" And they point, always with a kind smile on their face, and a laughter that sounds a little bit like the French people in the back kitchen watching us eat snails. And then, there it is, right over the Rivoli Bridge: the façade of an old baroque church, right next to McDonald's: Chiesa San Bartolomeo, which I think means Cheese Sandwich for Bart. We walk in and our world is transformed from hectic struggle for long pants to the serenity of marble, Renaissance art and classical architecture at its most exquisite. It is so beautiful that we all want to weep; or at least Sue and I do. Lara wants to know if she can go next door to McDonald's. The program is Corelli, Mozarti, and of course, Vivaldi.

We find our seats. The rustling of chairs subsides. The Holy Virgin looks down upon us from the vastly vaulted and domed ceiling, and a small door opens off the little stage in front. Eight men and women walk out ceremoniously, all dressed in black, all quite serious. They sit. Tune their violins, violas, cellos and harpsichord. The leader raises his violin, and they begin to play. For the next hour we listen to a couple of minor pieces by Corelli and Mozart, and then they play Vivaldi's Four Seasons in its entirety.

We've all heard bits and pieces of the Four Seasons, mostly in elevators, but I have never heard the entire work. It was breathtaking. The most exquisite chamber music I have ever heard, played in a vigorous, authentic, no-bullshit Italian style that made up in vibrancy, gusto and celestial acoustics whatever it may have lacked in modern day North European nuance. My goodness, there we were again, our lucky, lucky family, being blessed together by the best that heaven and earth have to offer, even if my cuffs were slipping a little.

The next day we took the train from Venice to Salzburg, Sue's favorite city, her home away from home, the place where Mozart and she studied and learned first-hand just how alive the hills really are with the sound of music. On the train, as we began to enter the grand stately presence of the Austrian Alps, Sue, quietly at first, gradually began to cry. Lara was the first one to see her weeping and was a little shocked. She said she had never seen Mommy cry quite this way before. Sue's emotional response to her "homeland" grew stronger; from a simple sentimental sniffle at first to a deep, full chested release, as she recalled the feelings she has so often savored here in these mountains from which she has for so long been separated. You could just see it in her face, the total relief and natural thankfulness that comes to one when after a long and contentious absence the sudden realization is at hand that "home" is only a few moments away. Sobbing, she says, "It's just so beautiful." And then she gasps for another breath.

When one looks out the window of the train and really sees them for the first time, the word splendor comes to mind; then wonder, holy and god. The mountains diminish in some ways the grandeur of the churches and castles and other monuments built in tribute to man-made things; even the great imaginative abstractions like freedom and brotherhood pale slightly by comparison. They stand over us like; well like the force of nature they are, the gentle, benevolent, deeply green force of nature they truly are. There is an earthly certainty about them, a certainty and promise and grace that Sue understands and feels inside of herself like the fluttering wings of her own personal angels.

And so she cries. Who wouldn't? And Lara stares, first out at the Alps and then at her mom. Sue is right: the majestic height and massive forms press against you, permeate your barriers, your European walls, so to speak (so many stone walls) and enter your heart, forcing you to breathe a little deeper. The benevolent green hues, the softness, the peace. In the middle of summer the peaks are still capped with snow. Down the slopes run vigorous fresh-water streams that one can follow to the valley below where villages have formed like the gathering of daffodils in a poem by Wordsworth. It's really quite stunning and even Lara is taken by it. "Isn't it beautiful, honey?" "Uh huh!" Lara responds in that tone that means in kid talk, yes Mommy it is truly a splendid thing to behold, but where are the kids?

Everything in Salzburg is easy. Changing money in the train station. Getting a taxi. Finding your hotel. Talking to people. And the scale of the old part of the city is perfect. There are no cars allowed. It is totally strollable and quaint and yet very interesting culturally. Makes the French look like Italians by comparison. "We gotta show Lara some baroque," I say in the taxi on the way to the hotel.

Later we are all very tired from the train ride and saddened by the thought of my leaving the following day. Sue and Lara are staying in Salzburg, but I must return. In ten years I have never been away from the office for more than a week, and the message machine is bursting. "I want to avoid a sad departure," I say. "So let's focus on the wonderful trip that we have had, the wonderful things we have done together, instead of on the sad stuff, like I have to leave tomorrow." We're in a booth and I slide over closer to Lara and place my arm around her. She has her sad face on, but I don't think she's being manipulative. I love her so much. I look at her and even to this day, after ten years of life together, ten years during which we could count the number of days I have been away from her on my two hands; yet even to this day sometimes I have a hard time absolutely believing she is here next to me. I just look at her face and think, what a miracle. Something is going on in our lives, all of our lives, about which we know really very little. It's all poetry and mystery and imagination: love I mean, and affection and the laughing we do together.

I start to review many of the fun things we have done. The amusement park in Paris that was right next to the Monet exhibit. The climb to the top of the Eiffel Tower. The walk along the Seine with her on my shoulders. The threat to throw her in if she didn't toe the mark. The fun we had with Fernando and

Sonia, Karla and Luka. Peeing, pooping, and picnicking in the Pyrenees. Quatro Gatos (Four Cats), the cool restaurant in Barcelona. The night train to Andorra. So many experiences we've had together. Lara nibbles at her schnitzel. It was in Salzburg that she actually discovered the "lollipop" configuration of our trip. "Look," I say. "We made a full circle." She says, "No." I say "Huh?" She says, "We didn't make a circle, we made a lollipop." Then she shows how the trip began in L.A., not Paris and how the trip from L.A. to Paris and the one from Paris to L.A. makes the stick of a lollipop.

And then I struck on it. A way to cheer her up: "Meowing Vivaldi." I started to meow like a cat the key phrases from the Vivaldi concert we had heard in Venice. Meow Meow, Meow Meow Meow Meow. Meow Meow Meow Meow Meow. It was very funny. Lara soon jumped in and we were Meowing Vivaldi together. The next thing you know we are outside the restaurant in one of Salzburg's big center squares with a big statue of Mozart and we are doing one of his piano concertos in DuckQuack and DogBark; Beethoven in ChickenSquack.

The next morning we take a walk and exchange some money and then it is time for me to leave. Sue and Lara meet me at the hotel. I sit down on a window sill and take Lara in my arms, hug her tightly and place her next to me. It is such a simple inconsequential moment and yet it is moments like this one, sitting on the window sill in Salzburg with my daughter next to me, holding on to me in sadness and love and good humor—it is moments like these that provide the answers to all the questions Spinoza and Kant may have had about human kind, about what we're here for, about purpose and destiny and redemption and all those other things. I look at Sue standing there, almost as sad as Lara. And I feel it deeply inside of me. In fact I think I even say it: "I am so lucky to have such wonderful people to love."

And that is our Christmas wish for all of our friends and neighbors and the awesome people with whom we are so privileged to work: that the love and forgiveness that Jesus posited so forcefully over 2,000 years ago—it remains the most radical proposal ever made, and the single most important evolutionary act to have taken place in modern times (since 25,000 B.C. anyway)—we want that love and forgiveness to become as deeply true and felt inside of you as it was for us in the moment we shared on the window sill in Salzburg. As one who never thought we would survive the sixties, let alone make it to the second millennium, it is something of a conversion for me to feel so optimistic about the long-term future, which is really more Lara's future than mine. But so much has been achieved since then—think Civil Rights, Human Rights, Cold War, South Africa, Israelis, Palestinians and now Syrians, Catholics and Protestants in Northern Ireland—so much has been accomplished that the possibility for a better world, with better people and more fulfilled lives, just seems more doable now, at the beginning of the NEW MILLENNIUM, than ever before. A little bit of Heaven is just as likely to show up around the next bend on our journey as the Armageddon some people are projecting. But we must keep our eye on the "Star" and "Believe" as fiercely as we do say, during a pennant race. Preparation in a situation like this is, of course, the key to success. And who better to look to than Jesus, on the 2,000th anniversary of his rather momentous birth, for the best way to get ready for "paradise." Remember this one?

> "Unless you become as a child, you cannot enter into the Kingdom of Heaven." — Jesus

Pretty clear. It's what Christmas is all about, which brings us to our long overdue close. We changed our minds. We want you ALL to know that we were joking about the food thing. If civilization really does crumble (which could be kind of fun as long one can get still get a limo), we invite you all over to the trailer for dehydrated chicken cordon bleu and a glass of sand. Mi trailer tu trailer, so to speak. Jesus would have wanted it that way.

With our most childish love,

Sue, Mark and Lara

1999
Important Events

- **The euro currency is established and the European Union is officially born.**

  Just in time for Y2K and the end of civilization.

- **NATO launches air strikes against Yugoslavia.**

  Lara floods the bathroom.

- **Supreme Court rules 5-4 that public schools are liable for failing to stop sexual harassment by students.**

  Dylan falls in love with Lara.

- **Columbine!**

- **Boris Yeltsin resigned as president of Russia, leaving Prime Minister Vladimir Putin as acting President.**

  Russia is a Republic now. A free country like us. Nothing to worry about!

- **Dow hits 10,000.**

  Family celebrates Lara's 10th year living inside a bull market. Daddy issues buy order.

The Year of the Empty Core

Mark, Sue, Lara and Fergie
Orange County, California

December 10, 2000

Dear friends, family and celebs,

Dare I say it? Dare I utter the words? I can feel myself biting my lip like Bill Clinton just before he feels our pain or parses one of his false equivocations. It just makes me nervous to think about it. I mean it's here. It's upon us. There's nothing we can do to stop it. And no. I don't mean the impending presidency of George W. Bush. Ugh! It's not that. It's the other words. Oh, the heck with it, Mark: Just say it: Merry Christmas. There. I've done it. I've said it: Merry Christmas. Yes: Merry Christmas. Happy Hanukkah. Joy to the World! Salam Allah Kum. I mean we're all about Kwanza, here in our house! And what else? Ashanti, I guess. So yes: Christmas makes me nervous.

There are a couple of reasons. First, of course, is the fact that I'm not ready. I feel the obligations swelling up like a bad sprain and I'm just not ready. Here's an example. Lara's in sixth grade now, and her teacher gave her an assignment to design the perfect holiday decorating scheme for the exterior of her house. "Let your imagination run wild," he tells the class, without the slightest consideration for what their extravagant sixth-grade abandon might mean to us, to parents and our shrinking life expectancy. Mega-lights. Arctic effects. Santa and his reindeers on the roof, plus real wise men and the Star of Bethlehem somehow dangling over our house from the heavens. I mean, from what am I going to hang the star? Lara showed me her drawing, and said, "This is how I want our house to look this year, Daddy."

God knows I want to be a good daddy. I want Lara to feel good about herself and her place in the community. But Jesus! The Army Corps of Engineers turned me down, flat. Said they might be able to get that many lights up on the house, but there was no way the structure would support a herd of reindeer and the "Bubba" guy. "Try the people who decorate the malls," they said.

I sit down with Lara and her drawing and I try to explain about structural tolerances and wattage. She looks up at me. Now that she's eleven, she has acquired an altogether new style of defiance, and it comes to you in a look, a particular kind of glance, which she shot up at me. I took another look at the drawing and grimaced at the manger, which included the entire population of people and farm animals from the little town of Bethlehem. I shook my head. "But Lara!" She gave me the look and pointed across the street to our neighbor's house.

Right! That's another thing that makes me nervous: The fierce competition to "out decorate" houses in the neighborhood. The contest began the day after Thanksgiving. I don't know where people find the time, but even as we were picking the last few crushed cranberries out of the carpet and the sun was setting over our sated, gurgling abs, the neighborhood suddenly began to glow like the Las Vegas strip. When I drive down the street now, I find myself looking for a marquis with Siegfried and Roy; or Frank, Dean and Sammy flashing on and off like roadway warnings. How did they get so many lights up so quickly, I wondered? Manny and Arlene's house always wins the contest, at least in terms of candle power, which is the scale used to measure the brightness of stars and galaxies. If Manny accidentally leaves his lights on during the day, for example, then you can't see the sun. UFOs land in our neighbor-hood during the holidays because they think Arlene's place is the signal they've been waiting for. And just to show you how interdependent the world has become as globalization sweeps over one meridian after another, when Arlene turns on her lights, the city of Shanghai and the state of Utah go black. Now, how am I supposed to compete with that?

So you can see how I could get a little nervous as the holiday season slouches toward us? Gift anxiety is another big problem. Not for friends and relatives, because we don't have any friends except you, and we don't know which trailer park our relatives are living in this season. But I have to buy gifts for my clients, and for the neighbors, and of course for Sue and Lara. What to buy? I kneel and pray. Yes! Thank you, Lord. Prayer answered. Sue's done. I'm going to get her a signed photograph of David Boies, the attorney that argued Al Gore's case before all those judges. Sue loves this guy. She has been thoroughly captivated by the strange, aberrant and to me very ominous election. (Just one more example, as far as I am concerned, of the vertiginous state that befalls a people who have nothing more ennobling to contend with than peace, prosperity and the quest for pharmaceutical entitlements.) But, hey: who listens to me?

Sue of course wants all the votes to be counted, and she has been carefully following the legal arguments that have usurped our family dinner-minute (used to be the family dinner-hour, but that's like so five minutes ago). "There is a big difference," Sue points out to me, "between interpreting the law and creating it. The Florida Supreme Court was obliged by statute and precedent to square the conflict between the statute that states the election must be certified at a specific date and the one that says that if there's a chance that it would change the outcome of an election, a hand count must be conducted. The court was not creating law. They were simply interpreting it, as they were obliged by their august positions to do." Whoa! I think about this, hard. "You're right," I say, a little bewildered. And then, pursuing the dialectic to the next level I say, "But where does Boies get those shirts; from Barbara Bush?" And that hair! I'm thinking constitutional amendment on the hair. I mean these are the people who are doing the bidding of the people who own our country, and it's like GQ didn't even exist. Anyway, I think that one of the reasons our marriage has remained so strong over the years is because Sue and I continue to engage in this kind of candid, meaningful dialogue.

Actually, what to buy the neighbors isn't that hard either, because Lara and I came up with a plan. To save money this year, she and I ordered the Christmas 2000 cookie making kit from the Williams-Sonoma catalog, and we plan to make cookies for everyone. We ordered the snowflake cookie kit and the alphabet cookie kit, which included icing pens, glitters, decorating sugars and something called dragees. You ever heard of those? Me neither. According to William-Sonoma, they're inedible silver-colored sugar decorations that have adorned cakes for generations throughout Europe. "The sine qua non for holiday cookie making." Lara asks why anyone would make sugar inedible. I say, hey, "sine qua non Lara," and we cough up an extra $475 dollars for the dragees; total cost for both cookie kits: $3495.00 shipping included. Our plan is to personalize the cookies by spelling out each neighbor's name, and wrapping them up with a dragee-covered snowflake in colorful festive boxes. The problem, of course—

and this really adds to my gift anxiety—is figuring out exactly what our neighbors' names are.

Wait. Here's some breaking news. As I sit typing away on my Yuletide greeting, I hear Sue groan downstairs. I think, my god! I haven't heard her agonize like that since she looked out the window at Arlene's Christmas lights. I run downstairs. What is it, honey, I inquire with authentic spousal concern. "The circuit court in Florida just ruled that those absentee ballot applications the Republicans took home and worked on were no problem. They're going to let them stand." I take her in my arms. "Oh, honey, I'm so sorry," I say. And then I think, shirts. It was the shirts!

Oh well. We're not going to let politics ruin our Christmas. "Lara, honey! Let's get to work on the cookies."

While Lara is getting the cookie kits out of the vault, I can finish up with our family news for the year. My goodness, what a year it has been for us. Lara learned how to whistle. Sue's been on a sabbatical. And guess what? In one year I got a colonoscopy and a literary agent, if you can believe that. I'll tell you all about it, but let's begin where we left off last year. Remember? The Millennium? The Finale? Boy was the end of civilization a big disappointment to us.

There we were on December 31, all dug-in in the trailer we purchased in the Mojave Desert, our credit cards shrewdly maxed out, waiting comfortably for the power grids to falter and panic to spread throughout the world. Lara, Sue, Fergie and I were in front of the TV, wrapped up in our warm, cozy militia-wear, all ready to gloat, when, instead, we witnessed the Millennium pass from one time zone to another as peaceful and uneventful as a mild weather front. Adding insult to injury, ABC offered the whole Millennium Celebration on video before it even got to us in Pacific Standard Time. L.A. didn't even get to be in the video. "Too boring," said some Roone Arledge-type guy. "Does this mean we have to return Disneyland?" Lara asked. (I had told Lara that Disneyland would soon be ours.) "Looks that way, sweetheart," I said, as I turned and dialed the *Trailer Trader*. "Yes, I'd like to place a classified ad, please. Just say 'A well-armed desert bunker in mint condition, dehydrated food and booby traps included.' "Oh, well. It was a little disappointing, but deep down we were actually glad we could still order pizza and have indoor plumbing and stuff. Our friends who had come out to the desert to survive with us (about fifty families), immediately got back in their SUVs and drove to the city to try to get their pets back. After they left, Sue, Lara and I laid back and became very philosophical. "I guess we have to go on living, then," I mused.

And that's what we did. We went back home and began working on Lara's State Report. As most of you know, every fifth grader in America (and I think China and Thailand, too) has to select a state, and then the parents of that child have the responsibility of working their butts off for months to create a thorough report on that state, including natural resources, industry, government, state bird, celebrities that live there and of course any connections with the budding Russian Mafia. Lara chose New York because that's where Broadway is located and Lara wants to be a Broadway star. Sue says, "Great. Let's take a trip to New York then." I stutter, trying to come up with some valid objections, like what about work? "We're professionals. We can't just up and go to New York." And, "What happens when we have to do her report on Ancient Civilizations? Are we just going to pack up and go to Egypt?" Sue grins. Before I form my oral arguments, she and Lara are packed, and the limo is pulling up to the curb.

We arrived at Newark airport via Pittsburgh (Sue bought our tickets from Priceline.com. which requires that all flights land at least once in a city no one wants to go to.) It was late at night (Priceline also stipulates that no landings can occur any time before twelve midnight.) But that was ok. As we drove from New Jersey to Manhattan, we could see the famous skyline silhouetted by the city lights and punctuated beautifully by the unmistakable spires of the Chrysler and Empire State Buildings. I'd been to the city many times during my peripatetic youth and my work for peace in the Middle East, but Sue hadn't been there for years, and it was the first time for Lara. Both of them were just thrilled. The cab turned a corner and we headed down to the tunnel. "We're going to take the Lincoln Tunnel under the East River, sweetheart," I explained in a seasoned tone to Lara. "And when we come out we'll be in New York City! Won't that be cool?" "Hudson River, Dad" she says. "We're going to take the Holland Tunnel under the Hudson River. The East River's over on like the 'east' side." "Whatever!" I say, authoritatively.

Our ten star hotel (the Essex House) was right on Central Park South, which is a great location (Thank You, Priceline.) It's right across the street from Central Park, two blocks from the Plaza, and three from Lara's favorite NYC destination: FAO Schwartz. There's a very famous children's book called *Eloise* about a rich eight-year-old girl who spends her entire life inside an elevator at the Plaza Hotel. I had read the book many times to Lara, as a way to familiarize her with all the things in life that she will never have. So we actually booked ourselves into the Plaza for the last two days of our stay (Compliments of American Express Bonus Buying Triple Coupon Award Points Program). In the crisp early morning hours, Sue and Lara and I took our first walk together in the Big Apple, strolled down Central Park

South from the Essex House to the Plaza. My gosh! How lucky I felt to have Sue and Lara in my life. If it weren't for Sue and her spontaneous determination to do the illogical thing, I'd be home fixing the paper feed mechanism on my laser printer instead of here, arm-in-arm against the cold metropolitan wind, piqued with excitement and anticipation, while aglow and flowing about a nanometer below the surface was our deep abiding love for one another. Without Lara, of course, there would never have been a state report to compel us here in the first place. On our return, we gratefully ordered hamburgers from room service at about two a.m., and were asleep by three.

The next thing I know, I hear Lara yelling something I don't quite understand. Still dazed, I shake my head and pry open my eyes. Lara has pulled the heavy drape away from the window and when I peer outside I see this lovely, snowy-white mist slowly descending onto the alley, transforming the scene into something edgeless and ethereal, so soft and unique that even the homeless people asleep on their cardboard looked like figures from a fairy tale. "It's snowing!" Lara sings. And Sue was just as thrilled. "It's snowing in New York!" she said. "What a wonderful omen."

Ooops! More breaking news. I'm right in the middle of my New York story when I hear Sue once again, downstairs. "Honey! Honey! Come here. Listen to this!" I haven't heard her this excited since Lara got the part of Alice in the play *Alice in Wonderland.* I run down stairs. "The Florida Supreme Court has ruled that the vote counting can continue. They're going to count the votes!" And I think, sure: they ought to count the votes. It's a close election. In a close election, they should take a second look at things. If we can clone a cow we ought to be able to count a few votes in a fair and equitable way. We look at Boise, who is being interviewed on all the cable news outlets and I'm thrilled by this guy's vice-like grasp of the law and his Napoleonic sense of strategy, but I'm also worried. I don't say this to Sue, but I'm thinking to myself, didn't I see that tie on a guy in Rumania back in '83? It may have passed muster in Tallahassee, but will it get past Sandra Day O'Connor?

The snowfall was an auspicious meteorological event; our entire stay in NYC was simply charmed. In no time at all, the three of us were dressed and strolling through Central Park, faces raised to meet the icy manna from on high. And the cool thing was that it only snowed for about half the day, and then the sun came out, which meant we could still tour the city and see the sights.

We walked down to Rockefeller Center, where Olympic-class skaters were performing on the famous ice rink. We watched. We videoed. We thought: yes, totally charmed. Even Katie Couric and Matt Laur were there, but that was a little strange. Have you noticed lately how fiercely the celebs are competing for the attention of common people like you and me? Whatever happened to that healthy contempt for the masses? Matt had an accordion and a little trained monkey who did funny things with the crowd, and Katie was actually eating fire off a torch. We think we even saw that Bryan whatever-his-name-is from CBS writing slurs about Diane Sawyer with a piece of chalk on the wall next to the NBC entrance. And Diane Sawyer herself was there poised before a crowd of people from St. Paul, pretending to be an apparition. But hey, I grabbed Lara and Sue and blew out of there. In my opinion, when celebs start acting like carnival people, it's time to move on. So we grabbed a cab to the Empire State Building. In no more than an hour and a half, we'd ripped six or seven feet through dense Manhattan traffic. Then we got out and walked. On the elevator to the top, I said some funny things to entertain the other people in the car. "It would have saved everyone a lot of trouble if King Kong had just taken the elevator." The folks in the elevator chuckled (as I knew they would) and I thought to myself, maybe I should do some standup while I'm here in the Apple. Maybe give Conan a call. But then I noticed Lara staring up at me with a blank, uncomprehending look. And I was shocked. She had no idea who King Kong was. "You've never seen King Kong?" I inquired. The crowd gasped. I looked at Sue. "Why hasn't this girl seen King Kong," I said accusingly. I always do this to Sue. Whenever I find a flaw in Lara's development (like if she doesn't know who translated *The Trial* into English, or missed one of the symbols in the Periodic Table of the Elements) I look piercingly at Sue and accuse her of stuff that normally leads Child Services to remove the child from the home. "How is this child supposed to understand New York City if she's never seen King Kong? I mean I thought we were doing research here?"

Once we got up there, Wow! What a view. The top of the Empire State Building is the only place in New York City where one can really be sure about the location, or even the existence of the East River. "There it is," I said proudly to Lara. "The East River." "New York Harbor, Dad!" Lara said with an irritating, eleven-year-old accuracy and nonchalance. Another thing we found out while we were up there is that it wasn't until the early American Indians actually climbed to the top of the famous edifice and looked around that they realized how much waterfront property they had given away. Needless to say, the chief was pretty pissed off at the agent who brokered the deal. "You mean we sold the entire island to the Stewy Vescents for a few beads and a Teflon pan," he screamed (By the way, this was the actual historical event that gave rise to the term "red man."). Of course the agent's lawyer stepped forward with signed disclosures and disclaimers, and it's basically been that way for the American Indian ever since. New York Harbor was the gateway to the Hudson River, down which flowed the bounty of early commerce like furs and food and Jewish comics. Whoever controlled the gateway, controlled the commerce. Lara and I discussed the strategic significance of the island to the development of the state of New York, and of course I summarized the lecture with a little scripture that is still familiar to all of us today. "Verily, Verily I say unto you, Location, Location, Location!"

Ok. Big surprise. Breaking news. "Honey! Oh my God, Honey. Come down here, quick!" I hear my wife yelling with a frustrated edge to her normally loving, euphonious voice. Once again, I leave my Christmas greeting and run downstairs. Of course by now, you all know exactly what I saw and heard. Boise, wearing a tie that was definitely made in Lahore, standing before the cameras telling us about the U.S. Supreme Court ruling that disallowed any chance of counting the votes. Poor Lara. Every one of the kids in her class was for Bush. "Their parents told them that Gore wants to forbid kids from playing video games until they're twenty-one," said Lara. "That's not true is it, Daddy?" "No, sweetheart. Sometimes grownups don't tell the truth, but of course if you tell a lie, we will take away all your toys and make you watch CSPAN," I explained judiciously. Lara had told her class that if Bush won, our family was going to move to Europe, which is what we had been bellowing tastefully in front of the T.V. for a week. But now with the market so far south, we'll probably have to head that way, too: we're thinking maybe Trinidad. Oh well. It's over, finally. And I'm glad. Last year: the end of civilization. This year: the end of democracy. Hey, life goes on.

And so did we. From the Empire State Building we made our

way down to the World Trade Center and Battery Park. It was about five o'clock by the time we reached the water, and we just missed the last tour boat to the Statue of Liberty. But that was ok, because a few yards down the wharf the Staten Island Ferry was just getting ready to embark on its short journey across the harbor. We ran down the boardwalk, and along with a very large crowd of what appeared to be people with jobs, we hopped on the ferry. Once on board, the first thing I did was to explain the concept of "job" to Lara. I used my dad as an example. Not only had he had a job, but my father was also born on Staten Island to an Italian immigrant dad and a Scotch/Irish mom, and so it was also a great opportunity to talk with Lara about her ancestors, patriarchy, the importance of bootleggers to the growth of the state and of course a word or two about the innate superiority of males. After the lecture, the first mate was kind enough to bandage the wounds I received from both Sue and Lara, who held an entirely different point of view.

The trip back to Manhattan was picture postcard perfect. A soft early twilight cast an ethereal light over the entire harbor. The sky was clear, the air was brisk and Lara, Sue and I stood on the bow (or was it the stern? Not sure? How do you tell on a ferry?); anyway, we stood out there on the front of the boat holding on to one another as the sea breeze blew back both of my hairs and we looked up and there she was: the lady of liberty towering over us with her eternal beacon of freedom and the inalienable rights of the individual. It was chillingly beautiful, and certainly one of the highlights of our trip, all the more so because we were able to witness and feel the moment together. As the Statue receded, the dramatic Manhattan skyline rose up before us like a medley of song from Sinatra and Nelson Riddle.

When we got back to the City, we decided to have a drink at

the top of the World Trade Center, but get this: they said I had to have a tie. Can you believe that? I complained to the guard (who they referred to as the Maître d') that I owned Microsoft stock and some Sun Microsystems. "I buy high and sell low," I said. "It's suckers like me that make the World Trade Center possible, and I can't even go up and have a drink?" The guard, glancing at Sue and Lara with what appeared to be a New York version of pity and compassion, said, "After five, sir, one must dress." Like what? I'm naked here? Tank tops aren't clothes? This aberrant, pretentious anachronistic custom seemed to prevail throughout the city (they made me wear a coat in the Oak Room at the Plaza, too), and although I must admit that Mayor Giuliani had done an admirable job cleaning up the city and turning what had been a rather seedy and threatening Times Square area into something that now resembles Toon-Town, New Yorkers still had a lot to learn about the moral superiority of cut-offs over Brooks Brothers.

At night, of course, we went to shows. It was so cool to be able to grab a cab and in five minutes be at the theater. Here in Southern California, if you want to get to the theater, you have to take a vacation day. Like the rest of the world, Lara was captivated by the size and spectacle and intriguing possibilities of Broadway, which has ten times the imaginative power of a Hollywood or Vegas or even a Branson, Missouri. We saw The Lion King, by Elton John, Aida by Elton John, a new Tosca by Elton John and a modern musical version of The New York Times Classified Ads by (you guessed it) Elton John and Tim Rice, again. There were lots of revivals, too; and I think Sue and Lara caught them all: The Music Man, Annie Get Your Gun, Beauty and the Beast. My tastes in theater tend to be a bit more serious; so I went to see Jackie Mason, the master of high Hebraic humor. That was really a weird experience. Except for me, the audience consisted of Jews and Italians, a perfect example of life imitating art. All the Jewish people had cushions under their arms because they knew the seats in the theater wouldn't be comfortable enough. All the Italian people sounded just like the Sopranos, and were all about getting tickets to Yankee games and threatening Mason with catcalls like, "Hey Jackie, you better make me laugh tonight." I also went to a play called *Copenhagen*. In spite of its droll-sounding thematics, it was superb. It was about a meeting between two nuclear physicists—Niels Bohr and Werner Heisenberg—during which they attempted to figure out whether scientists should be held morally accountable for the things they invent, like thermonuclear bombs and stuff. In spite of the "uncertainty" that was at the core of the piece, it turns out: yes, if you lose the war, and no if you win.

Toward the end of our visit to the City, I called my agent at ICM to arrange a meeting. I don't think I've told the story about my agent. Boy, talk about Christmas. This was Christmas with a capital "C." Listen to this. Back in January I sent a copy of the Christmas Letter 2000, the one about the end of civilization, to Kurt Andersen at the *New Yorker Magazine*. He's quite a respected writer/entrepreneur in New York who had written a fine novel about the convergence of high technology, mass media and Wall Street. It's called *Turn of the Century* and he'd love for you to buy a copy for everyone in your zip code. I told Kurt I felt that the Christmas Letter was a much-neglected literary form and that I had taken on the challenge of rehabilitating the genre, of raising it to the pantheon of gilded letters to which it belonged. He laughed. Said I was a fine, funny writer, but didn't know what one might do with a Christmas Letter as a literary form. Then he suggested that I send a copy to his agent. So I did. Suzanne called me on St. Patrick's Day and said the material—being all my funny, charming (not to mention "deep") Christmas letters since 1990—had merit and that it should be edited tastefully into a book; that if I did so, she would try to sell it. Whoa! I was so excited, but anxious, too. The word "tastefully" really threw me. You have to remember that Suzanne is not just any Suzanne. She's Suzanne the literary agent with International Creative Management (ICM). She represents Kurt Andersen, Spalding Gray, Caleb Carr and lots of other writers who either are or would like to be short-listed for the Nobel Prize, or at least a spot on BookTV. Since you and most of the other people who read my Christmas Letters don't really know how to read that well (thus the limited use of words over four syllables), this probably won't mean much. But movie stars you know. And ICM (the Hollywood office) represents people like Julia Roberts, Mel Gibson, Michelle Pfeifer, Tim Robbins and Darren Aronofsky. That tells you something, right? So Suzanne, my agent Suzanne, is like what? Yes. There's no other word. She's like an angel, like an angel who does not return your calls, but an angel nonetheless.

Before leaving the City, I called Suzanne at her office on West 57th (just a block from the Plaza Hotel where I was still trying to borrow a coat and tie so I could eat breakfast). Her assistant Caroline answered and told me that Suzanne had just caught a flight to the west coast. Shoot, I think to myself. Someone must have told her I was coming.

We spent a week in NYC; days devoted to fun and culture, nights to Elton John. Then we rented a car and drove north to Albany to show Lara the capital. On the way we were able to visit all the historical landmarks related to the Revolutionary War, like Valley Forge, Fort Ticonderoga and the place where Bob Hope and the Andrew Sisters entertained the Revolutionary Army just outside Poughkeepsie.

Wonderbear met us in Albany. Wonderbear (it's his real name, by the way) and Sue had studied German literature in Salzburg, Austria back in the seventies. While trying to translate Hoffmansthall into English, the two of them got so drunk that after thirty years neither one has quite sobered up yet. For Wonderbear it doesn't matter that much, because he's a lobbyist. For Sue either, actually. She's in education and her breezy, slightly besotted nature is viewed as an endearing caprice. Wonderbear showed Lara all the important sites in Albany and introduced us to Governor Pataki (well, not Pataki, but the guy that alters his pants). Later, he took us to a big resort on Lake George where he had the twelve-star restaurant prepare an extraordinary feast. Wonderbear is a connoisseur of fine wine and cuisine. He had selected each of the six bottles of vintage wines from his own personal cellar, and these wines were so precious that the chef actually tailored a separate course for each bottle. Sue and I were used to selecting a wine that compliments the meal, like a nice Boone's Farm '99 with our bucket of ribs, but in this case the process was reversed. One selected the wine, and the kitchen prepared a meal that would bring closure to the august libation. I could tell we were in for a real treat, and gave Wonderbear one of the highest forms of praise a gourmet host can receive. "These cheeses don't even stink much" I exuded. "Usually French cheeses stink like feet, don't you think? Hey, a rhyme!" Sue grimaced, as the ritual opening of the bottles began. Seconds before we heard the ceremonial pop from the first bottle, however, I received a note from the Maître d'. It said, "Emergency. Please call home immediately."

And that was that: Trip over. Sue's mom had slipped and broken her hip back in Orange County, and after some haggling on the phone with our friends at Priceline.com and twelve hours on the road back to JFK, we flew home. She's ok, now. In fact, she's great. Nana had always wanted a new hip. And hey: thanks to Priceline, the entire trip cost about half what we paid for the cookie kits, plus Lara totally aced her state report.

So here we are again: page twenty or so, and I'm only at about April. Well, take a break here. Return some gifts. Think up a resolution. Maybe try and figure out who Aronofsky is. Then come back and I'll tell you our family secret.

I think most families have secrets they hesitate to reveal to the outside world. Cousins who kill for fun, or become Republicans. That gold mine investment. College grades. The secrets usually lie deep within the genealogical chart or are concealed in old shoeboxes on the top shelf of the linen closet. We have one too. Ready? Ok. Here it is: We don't place our toilet paper on the roll dispenser anymore. We used to. After the last . . . well what else are you going to call it: wipe, we'd dutifully remove the empty cardboard core and place the new snowy white cylinder of two ply onto the axle and insert it properly back into the bracket. Done. Ready for the next movement, so-to-speak. But we don't do that anymore. And you want to know why? No time. Too busy. Phone's ringing. School starts in two minutes. Tennis lesson at three. Phone's ringing. Someone's at the door. Phone's ringing. See if this sounds familiar? "Will someone please get me a roll of toilet paper?" Thought so. We just feel rushed all the time now. So instead of taking the few moments required to properly replace the toilet paper, these days we just plop it on top of the dispenser, and it sits there like a portly Greek pillar, a strange scatological monument to our tragically hurried life and times. For me then, this year has been the Year of the Empty Core. And do you want to know what the main culprit is? Finding stuff. I'd say our family spends a good 75% of its time just finding stuff.

Example: Lara and I are working on the New York Report. We've colored the state flag, the state bird and the state animal. Now it's ten-thirty at night. The report's due tomorrow. And we've just begun to color the wings of the New York state insect (true story): the ladybug. "Where are my colored pencils?" I ask my little prodigy. "I don't know," she says nonchalantly. "What do you mean, you don't know?" I inquire sagaciously. "I mean I don't know," she responds irritatingly. From an outsider's view, this may seem innocent enough. A young, carefree ten-year-old girl says she can't recall where she put the colored pencils after she used them last. No reason for a grumpy fifty-two-year-old father to get upset about that. But that's the problem with outside perspectives, isn't it? People possessing them rarely have the deep penetrating insights necessary to make an informed judgment about something like this. They lack the historical data, the relentless accrual of moment and memory that grows over time to form what we might call an "attitude." In short, they don't know shit from Shinola. This was not the first time this has happened. "Where are your shoes?" "I don't know." "Where is your homework?" "I don't know." "Where is your hairbrush?" "I don't know." "Where did you put your math book?" "I didn't put it anywhere." "Toothpaste?" "Don't know." "Water bottle?" "Nope. Don't know." "Retainer?" "Can't find it." "Calculator?" "Haven't seen it." "My new mechanical pencil?" "Not me. Didn't use it." "My clear plastic ruler?" "The clear plastic one? I haven't seen that one for a while." "New fifty dollar sweater?" "Gone. Don't know what happened to it." "The dog?" "Don't know?" "The car." "Isn't it in the garage? If it's not there, I don't know." "Garage?" "Is that gone, too? Jeez! I don't know, Dad." I serenely take a deep, deep breath and launch an unconditional entreaty which causes all the dogs in the neighborhood to begin barking: "Find them!"

"Ok," she says. "Geeez! I think they're downstairs in the blue desk." She trots down the stairs and before the neighbors can get their robes on and go outside to disable their car alarms, Ouila! Colored pencils.

I think a lot of this absent-mindedness isn't absent-mindedness at all. It's more like genius and a unique pre-teen otherworldliness. Lara lives in quite a different universe than the one to which I, as a pseudo-adult, have been consigned. But twirling is a big factor, too. Yes. I said twirling. Lara is twirling herself through life these days. I walk into the kitchen in the morning to pop my first brewski and there she is: twirling around in her silk pajamas like a neon dervish. "How do you do that?" I ask her as she twirls herself a bowl of Rice Krispies. "What?" she asks, not even aware that she's making thirty-five, forty revolutions per minute with a carton of milk in one hand and a cereal box in the other. "Twirl like that?" I say, feeling myself begin to twirl a little bit, too. "Oh," she says, as she twirls over to the table. "I just love to twirl."

Ballet probably has a lot to do with it. Ballet of course is just a Russian form of twirling with French subtitles, and Lara's been taking lessons for quite a while. Like her heart and mind, Lara's body is also acquiring a new knowledge, the kind young knowing angels might possess without really being aware of it. I watch her dance and think: look at her all growing up so beautifully. I mean Geeez!

And speaking of growing up: check this out. Sue and Lara attended a "growth and development" tea at Lara's school this year. It was called a tea, but it was really a secret meeting about breasts. Once again: poor Lara. Because she is so bright, we put her into kindergarten when she was about six months old, and so she's always the youngest one in the class. Plus, she's in a class of brilliant girls and boys with off-the-chart intelligence and wit. Example: Deena takes her pet battery to school with her. She teaches her battery tricks at lunch. She collects "Made in China" tags. And makes up algorithms and then puts them to music for fun. And Michael, a perfectly normal, totally white eleven-year-old boy, when asked what he wanted to be when grows up answered, "I want to be the first black, woman president." Lara goes head-to-head with these kids, but most of them are at least a year ahead developmentally, and some are getting, yes: breasts. I can't imagine talking about puberty at a tea, but that's what they did. They showed "the film" on Growth and Development and Sue and I were so proud of Lara's mature response to these important issues. The first thing she said after getting home was, "That was disgusting."

"But it is totally natural," I responded with a wise, grown-up perspective way beyond my years. "We've been developing like this for over three million years." "Ha!" says Lara. "Boys don't do anything. They get a little hair under their arms. We get breasts! Hips! It's so disgusting. We're only kids," she concludes. "They shouldn't be scaring us like this." Then she twirls off to her room. We're keeping it a secret from her for now, but when Lara is a little older she'll understand that she needn't worry about breasts because by the time she gets them she'll be safely tucked away in the celibate religious order of her choice.

For now, however, let her enjoy this magical period of girlhood. Her mind is so active these days that it's hard to track. From one thing to another it darts like a hummingbird from flower to flower, sipping, tasting, expressing. "I just love glitter," she says while we're in a store called Zutopia, looking for a Roxy jacket to wear to camp. "It's just so shiny and bright and happy." And then she makes the shift that always jolts me out of adult creative thinking like, how many more miles can I drive before I have to buy new tires. "Why are streets black?" she asks. Huh? Streets? "Why are they always that boring black? Why not blue, a nice pretty blue." When I asked Lara if she was ever afraid of the dark, she said, "Oh yea. But when I get afraid, I try to remember Adrian's smile! (One of Lara's friends) And that always makes me feel better." And I think, how did she figure that out?

Lara and I read *Tom Sawyer* and *Huckleberry Finn* together this year. If you want to know what racism felt like before we had a word for it, read Mark Twain. Lara also auditioned for and got the role of Alice in *Alice in Wonderland*. Isn't it strange how when you watch your child performing on stage with twenty other kids, it seems like yours is the only one there? She ran for class Secretary. She didn't win, but she learned. And for the first time in her life, she toilet papered houses.

She and all her girlfriends snuck out late at night and papered the homes of all the boys in their class. It was a very strange night, because Sue and I were the getaway drivers. Imagine: eight girls in two cars, prowling at one o'clock in the morning through suburban neighborhood streets, then slinking out and tossing about eight hundred rolls of toilet paper up over the eaves and trees and roofs of the targeted boys. As they arched over the tops of the trees, the long streams of tissue would actually glow in the moonlight like expensive special effects. The girls left little calling cards on the porch that said, "TP Avengers," because less than a month had passed since the boys had "hit" the homes of the girls. As we stealthily sped away, I looked in my rearview mirror and was astonished by the pure white work of art that was left behind; luminous, deliquescent and stark as a wrap by the famous Christo. In the back seat the girls were carbonated with clandestine glee, as I nervously scanned the night sky for signs of police helicopters.

Lara exchanged her first e-mail this year. She got on the air with Radio Disney. We attended our first world-class Flamenco dance performance. Wow. Very powerful. The dancers were actually having sex by snapping their fingers, and if it wasn't good, they'd stamp their feet hard on the floor. Lara's internal life expanded to a new galactic dimension. And as I said in the beginning of our little Christmas epistle, she finally learned to whistle; something my dad passed onto me, and I to her.

As for Sue, she's home every day, working diligently six or seven minutes a day on the research for her Sabbatical. The rest of the time she devotes to driving me out of my mind by walking into the office just as I'm ready to solve a world problem like hunger or cost-effective fiber optic communications or creating a remote control that old people can use; just when the answer is percolating up through my inspiring mind, Sue walks in and asks me if I know where she put the new box of trash can liners. Huh? Trash can liners? No sweetheart. We hug. I start over. My achievements this year include getting up in the morning, learning how to twirl, finding things, publishing a few poems and editing all these precious Christmas letters into a charming little book which my agent at ICM will sell for at least as much as Hillary got for her dumb story.

As for Southern California news, what's the word they used during the court battles: trumped. We've been totally trumped by Florida. I mean we got no media coverage this year. But word is that our Secretary of State has notified all precincts throughout the state that from now on ballots from all of our elections are to be thrown into the dumpster. That ought to get us some media coverage. No, the only other thing I can think of that has happened here is Brad Pitt's marriage and Meg Ryan's break up.

Hey! I take that back. Here's some breaking news and it's from right here in Southern California. I just heard that on December 7th at 5:15 p.m. the state declared its first-ever Stage 3 power emergency. Is that cool? Looks like rates are going to go up about 30%. Well at least it's news. And guess what: December 7th. 5:15 p.m., precisely when Arlene threw the switch on her Christmas lights.

Ok, I better get this down. This is the end. What day was it? Thursday I guess, December 14. I think I had spent most of the morning trying to keep up with my work-in-progress, so I'm like furiously concepting, editing and converting the known universe into an MPEG file, when Sue walks up behind me and says, "Would you like to join your wife for lunch at Fashion Island?" Huh? Lunch? It was a beautiful day and she was going down there to do some—go ahead Mark, say it: Christmas shopping. We talked and decided to wait until Lara got out of school. "We'll pick her up, and then we can all have dinner together and view the tree." That's one of ostentatious conceits about shopping in Newport Beach: you get to stand at the base of the tallest decorated Christmas tree in the free world, stare up, and then go, "Jesus! Where'd they get this thing?"

So it's only about five o'clock, but Fashion Island is already packed with cars, and Lara and I spend a lot of time driving up and down the aisles in the parking lot looking for an empty slot. "There's Mommy," Lara yells. We see Sue walking by the storefronts on her way to the restaurant where we planned to have dinner. Lara puts her head out the window and continues to yell,

"Mommy! Mommy!" Sue crosses the street and walks toward us. Lara climbs out of the open window and into Sue's arms, while I continued to circle the vast, densely packed lot until I feel like a member of the Donner party. Before dinner, we all walk into the Sharper Image store to buy ionic hair brushes for Marsha, Mike and one other family member whose name I can't quite recall. Lara loves the Sharper Image store because there are so many cool gizmos to play around with: electronic drum sets, electronic tennis games, the electronic wallet, tree and spouse. Lara headed right to the electronic keyboard, and she figures out how to play the theme song to my most hated movie ever, *Titanic.* Sue and I walk around the corner and decide to buy her Mom a little fan that fits around the neck and keeps one cool, no matter how hot it gets. While Sue is paying for our gizmos, I sit down in this big leather chair that's imbedded with a series of little massage balls that respond to a remote control. Press the button and they massage your back from butt to C-spine. I'm really tired. A little spaced, too. And probably very low on blood sugar. So as the big chair begins to massage my back, the whole Sharper Image environment segues into something a bit surreal and even slightly psychedelic. But I could handle it, because I'd lived through the sixties, and that's really what the sixties did for people: prepared them to deal with the low blood sugar experiences of the 21st century. With our ionic brushes and electric neck fans under our arms, we left Sharper Image and went next door to a restaurant called Chimayo's. We got a table by the fireplace. That was nice, the three us: Sue, who always looks like an ideal to me, the reflection, manifestation, emanation or whatever of some Platonic ideal that has finally found a comfortable home in reality; Lara who is our reason for being; and me, a Platonic ideal downsized to a notion. The lights were down and the fire created a warm comfortable glow. We took off our jackets and began to scrutinize the menu. Unfortunately for us, Lara seems to have acquired biblical tastes. By that I mean her palate, like the road to heaven, is extremely narrow, and in the tradition of John the Baptist who ate nothing but locusts and honey, Lara has restricted her diet to three items: rice, beans and chocolate. We couldn't find anything on the menu that she'd eat, but the waitress offered to create a plate for her, with just some air on it. "Yes," she said. "I'll just have air." I ordered a chicken dish from the brick oven. Sue ordered a chili relleno from the appetizer menu. Then we made small talk about Christmas gifts, and the big tree that we were going to go see later.

While we were talking, Sue remembered that we were supposed to call Aunt Marsha and confirm her and Lara's trip to Sea World on Saturday. Happy for any excuse to withdraw from eating, Lara takes the cell phone. Sue recites the number to her from memory. Lara gets on the phone, and I listen to her side of the conversation, which seems a little formal. Lara and Marsha exchange comments for a little while, and then, surprisingly, Lara hands the phone over to me. "Aunt Marsha wants to talk to you," Lara says. This was supposed to be between the two of them, and I was a little upset with Marsha for abandoning the conversation with Lara so soon. "Hello," I said. "Hi," says Marsha. I can tell immediately that she is in serious mode. "Where are you?" she asks. "What do you mean?" "Where are you guys calling from?" "We're at Fashion Island. We're having dinner in a restaurant." "Are you sitting down?" "We're having dinner." "I don't want you to react right now, with Lara and Sue there, but I have some news."

My stomach tightens. My throat tightens. I think to myself, control yourself. Stay casual. I know something has happened to

Dad. I know my Dad is dead.

"Daddy died today," she says, choking back her own tears. I knew it! Inside I hear myself go fuck, fuck, fuck! But I reveal nothing. "Yea? What happened?" And she tells me that they are saying he had a heart attack. We'd been struggling with a cancer for six months, but he was fit. Things looked good. They were starting chemo. What the hell happened? And I listen to Marsha's description of the events which brought Daddy to his last moments on earth, his final moments of life, his end as a human being and his beginning as a new spirit, in a new realm, with an entirely new destiny before him. I ache inside. I am so mixed up. Waves of feeling sweep over me. No. This cannot be true. But this is true. This is so fucking true that I can't stand it. And at the same time I am glad this has happened because it has saved my father from so much suffering. I am glad. This is a good thing. But it is just not possible that he is gone. It is just not possible that I no longer have a father here. This cannot be. This death. This end. This goddamn heartless thing.

So Ok, now you have to be the tough guy, the strong male guy. Show no emotion. Talk about the tree. The big Christmas tree. Sue and Lara are at the table and I don't want them to hear about this here in public. I'll tell them later when we get home. So what are we going to get Chelsea for Christmas? I'm glad we brought our coats. Is that all you are going to eat? Anyone want desert? My Dad is dead. My father is gone, but I remain thoroughly calm and act as if we were talking about a new soup recipe. I tell Marsha that I will call her back later. And then I eat the vegetables and the cheddar cheese potatoes. I can't eat the chicken. I look at Sue and Lara. I listen to them talking, and once again I feel this deep, benevolent power surge up within me: how lucky I am, how lucky, lucky, lucky to have them in my life. Please help my father dear Lord. Please help my Dad.

Later that night I told Sue and Lara that my father had passed away. It began a long, aching week of sorrow, confusion and endless funeral arrangements, which is why our greeting this year has had to dissolve from a Merry Christmas to a Happy New Year. To quote from one of Sinatra's memorable tunes, "It's been a very good year." With a very sad ending.

Speaking of angels, I feel my father's passing somehow put us in closer touch with them, with the angelic order that I'm pretty sure surrounds us and lights our way through the dark night of our mortality, while helping us cope when people we don't like are happy and win stuff. To close our last Christmas letter, then: let me recall a summer night that gave way to that kind of angelic grace. I'm sitting on the floor of the family room, with the monthly bills spread out in front of me, listening to the voice of our neighbor, Steve Physioc, broadcast Fox Sport's play-by-play of the Angel's game on T.V. (Get it? "Angels" game) It's ten o'clock. I'm writing out checks. Sue's in bed, and I'm waiting up for Lara who has gone to church with our neighbors, "to see what it's like," she said, since we only go when we feel a big need to beg God for money. So it's quiet, and I'm sitting on the floor cross-legged, thinking to myself, Holy Shit! A hundred and thirty dollars for electricity?

Suddenly, I'm startled out of my deep meditation by the sound of the front door opening and then slamming shut. Huh? What? Angels? It probably sounds like a perfectly normal event to occur in a family household, the young daughter walking in after a night of prayer, but for me it became something remarkable. Lara burst in like a sudden light through the open door and twirled onto the tiled entryway with one blue and one yellow helium balloon bouncing in the air over her head. She was wearing a long, tailored pink dress with fine embroidery around the neck. She did a few spins and was ready to leap back-first onto the big blue sofa when I yelled, "Wait! Wait! Don't mess up my bills!" Lara laughed. I asked about the night.

"Booooring," she said, "Chelsea and I played rock-scissors-paper and guess-which-hand-the-penny's-in." We continued to talk, and I made a conscious effort to attend to Lara, to listen carefully to what she was saying. I know that sounds pretty obvious, but I think there is a tendency sometimes to short kids on attention, especially if they're telling you about the games they played while somber adults were praying for their very souls. As I listened, I also looked into her eyes and as I looked and listened I saw and heard something new, at least for me. Lara was in bloom. She was glowing from the inside out and even her mundane speech seemed tinged with a musical quality. I watched her face and noticed something that had probably been pretty obvious to Sue, who is a much better observer than I am, since the day she was born: Lara was becoming the person she was going to be. Beautiful. Confident. Capable. Funny. Intelligent, without being controlling. Innocent without being naïve. Responsive without being a sap.

I know it sounds lame to say that she was becoming the person she was going to be, because all kids are becoming who (Or is that, whom?) they will be, but saying it this way has a meaning for me that seems to fit the moment. What I felt that night as I watched and listened was something a notch above the norm. Lara, aglow in her simple reminiscence of games, was shimmering in front of me in her pink dress and blond hair, which she had unbound from the braid that Sue had worked it into. As she shook her head, I saw the future unfurl; not in a concrete clairvoyant way with time and space and events and stuff, but in a purely ineffable way; me fading away, and she ascending toward the stars, and as the stars recede taking her turn at being the sun. She was still a little girl who loved to play hide-and-seek and rock-scissor-paper, but her speech and her countenance were elevated that evening (I'm sure of it) to the place where angels are, where the wise ones are who look over us in their invisible way and whisper into the ear of our souls, "grow" "become" "rock out!".

And so this will have to be the last of our long—some say endless—Christmas letters. Since the wall paintings of Cro-Magnon Woman in the caves of Western Europe, since the ancient Egyptian hieroglyphics and Gutenberg's famous Christmas epistle about his daughter's dance recital, the Christmas letter has been a simple note about the growth and accomplishment of the kids. But as the kids grow and become more complex, it gets harder to capture them in stick figures and humorous quips, which is why humankind invented home movies. We began our family letter as a humorous way to recall for ourselves, friends and relatives (plus the famous people we are so desperate to meet), the spirit of our lives and times, year by year, one humbling incident after another over the last decade. Now the decade has closed, and soon—like in a few days—the millennium too will have reached its genuine end. If you got the letter back in '89, you'll recall the day Lara was born was the day the Berlin Wall came toppling down and the stock market began its historical decade run of the bulls, which just goes to show that one person, even a newborn, really CAN make a difference. A lot has happened since then, and most of the important stuff, like the lullabies we sang to Lara as an infant, how we redid our landscape, and the inspiring story of the six percent, 30-year fixed, are all in the letters. Of course historically, it has been a remarkable decade, too. (Actually, some say the 90's launched the beginning of the end of history, but nervous untenured historians throughout the country adamantly deny it, accusing university officials of inventing the idea as yet one more insidious way to cut costs.) In our view, history (or as Lara calls it: Herstory) is created moment by moment inside the house and around the neighborhood, at least that's where the herstory of the heart and soul is created, which is the one that counts. Some of those untenured historians agree, and have actually proposed removing the part about the Civil War (which is so depressing) from sixth grade social studies texts and replacing it with the story of Lara's quest to get through the decade without eating any food. As we bid adieu, then, to the decade and the twentieth century, we hope you will think of our little history as an attempt to connect with yours, because at the core of things, at "the heart," we are all united by our common heritage: the heritage of human beings getting through the day, and trying together to perhaps meet a celebrity or two.

Let us leave you then with our fondest wishes and blessings, and with these parting words for the new millennium; May you twirl through life with profound love and forgiveness (which is what Christmas should always be about).

May there always be paper on your roll
And may your agent return your call.
With our very best to you and all those you love,

Mark, Sue, Lara and Fergie

2000
Important Events

- **After surviving Y2K, the big question becomes: Is this the first year of the 21st century or the last year of the 20th?**

  Lara gets out her Gregorian calendar. Explains millenniums to parents.

- **The draft of the Human Genome Project announced at White House by President Bill Clinton, Francis Collins and Craig Venter.**

  Finally! Proof for Lara that family descends from famous people.

- **Green Day is big.**

  Lara trades in Dylan for Billie Joe Armstrong.

- **4th in series, *Harry Potter and the Goblet of Fire* released.**

  Daddy wants to know, "Who the hell is this Lord Voldemart?"

Acknowledgements

This book would not have been possible without inspiration and help from innumerable individuals. But since the word "innumerable" apparently means "countless," "incalculable," and "infinite," it would just be crazy to try to acknowledge them all.

But here are a few: First, I want to especially thank early paleolithic humans for their original Christmas Letter, which you can find on the walls of a cave in Lascaux, France.

And many thanks to the ancient Egyptians as well, without whom we would not have the letter "M". It was indispensable to the writing of this book.

The contribution of Johannes Guttenberg goes without saying. His movable type laid the foundation, not only for Kindle and the first printed Bible, but also for the first printed Christmas Letter, which told neighbors and family how much smarter his son Ralph was than any of the other kids in the city of Mainz.

Of course, I want to thank Mary and Joseph for obvious reasons.

More recently, a huge debt of gratitude goes to the capitalist economic system for making Christmas the blockbuster commercial success we know today, for destroying the true meaning of the holiday and getting people to buy stuff, including this book.

Dachshunds! Have we thanked dachshunds? We want to thank dachshunds for being so cute, even though it's hard to spell dachshunds. (Go ahead: try it.)

And what about the public school system? Thank you public school for taking care of Lara during the day while I worked on this book. We could not have done it without you, and for FREE!

Okay, not free. Thank you, Orange County taxes! And Prop 13!

Another person I need to salute is my wonderful agent, Suzanne. But I have neither seen nor heard from Suzanne since 2002. If anyone knows where she is, please call me.

A careful reading of this book will reveal a lot of psychological problems on the part of the author, and I want to extend my sincerest appreciation to all the therapists who helped me out while I was pretending to be a parent. Way too "innumerable" to name, let me just say thanks to the Jungians, Behavior Mod people and Mo, the only therapist I know who still believes in Santa Claus AND Electro-Shock.

We owe a huge debt of gratitude to the staff at Larissa Press, my loyal publishing house, which consists of me. Without this indefatigable and innumerable team of professionals the word "paleolithic" would never have been spelled correctly, not to mention the names of the Three Wise Men.

And we shan't forget the three wise men. These guys inspired me throughout the writing AND procrastination of this book. Whenever I got stuck I remembered their sagacious words. I can't remember them now. But a huge help, guys!

I would feel remiss if I didn't acknowledge the Mayans. I don't know if you recall our trip to Cancun back in 1999, but while standing at the top of the Mayan pyramid in Chichen Itza, Lara and I experienced a transcendent epiphany about our stock portfolio which led to returns sufficient to finance five years of drama instruction at the Laguna Beach Playhouse. Without the

Mayans, Lara may have ended up playing third string center fielder on Tiffany's, a girls' softball team, instead of starring in something fantastic that I can't recall right now. Go Mayans.

I mustn't go another minute without expressing my gratitude to snack food. What manna was to Israelites wandering in the empty desert, snack food is to writers staring at the wilderness of the empty page. The great thing is the innumerable variety of snacks available to a struggling writer today. The deep-fried, lavender flavored lint balls from the dryer got me through the chapter on chores. And while writing the acknowledgements themselves, I downed a whole bag of vanilla frosted pork rinds. So, thanks snacks.

But without question my greatest and most enduring benefactor has been my DNA, some of which I guess came from other people who I should thank. Without my DNA *The Christmas Letters* simply would not exist, and you'd have to read yet another book by David Sedaris.

And finally, no: we haven't forgotten Shark Tank, which has a 20% equity interest in this book.

As for anyone we may have forgotten, let me just say we didn't forget. You're just too innumerable. But thank you!

WILLIAMS-SONOMA

About the Author

Before winning the Nobel Prize for the second time, Mark Mendizza was a . . . wait! He didn't win the Nobel Prize. Forget that. . .

He was a commercial writer. Clients said it was the funniest stuff they'd ever read, even when it was about serious subjects like how to change a bicycle spoke. He spent the 70's recovering from the 60's. And the 80's he lived as an expatriate in the Middle East, where he had the whole region laughing about his recipe for peppermint kabob. Then he got serious. He started a marketing company; got married to Sue; and spent the 90's in love, raising Lara. When Wordsworth said, "The child is the father of the man," he had Mark in mind. His latest book is about the experience and deep meaning of the ordinary family. It's fun. It's touching. It's ridiculous. Hey, It's family.

There's more...

The Christmas Letters, II

Same Family – New Decade – More Hoots

With any luck, available November 2021

Yes. The saga continues.
More enchanting stories, hysterical drama and deep irrelevant thoughts.

Look for it on Amazon or your favorite bookstore.

Made in the USA
Monee, IL
26 September 2021

78778675R00138